IMAGES OF THE CIVIL WAR

IMAGES OF THE CIVIL WAR

THE PAINTINGS OF MORT KÜNSTLER
THE TEXT OF JAMES M. McPHERSON

GRAMERCY BOOKS

NEW YORK • AVENEL, NEW JERSEY

To Deborah, the best thing that ever happened to me.

Illustrations copyright © 1992 by Mort Künstler
Text copyright © 1992 by James M. McPherson
All rights reserved

This 1992 edition is published by Gramercy Books
distributed by Outlet Book Company, Inc.,
a Random House Company,
40 Engelhard Avenue,
Avenel, New Jersey 07001.

Designed by Liz Trovato

Printed and bound in the United States

Library of Congress Cataloging-in-Publication Data

McPherson, James M.
    Images of the Civil War / text by James M. McPherson :
illustrations by Mort Künstler.—1992 ed.
        p.   cm.
    ISBN 0-517-07356-0
    1. United States—History—Civil War, 1861-1865. 2. United States
—History—Civil War, 1861-1865—Art and the war. 3. United States
—History—Civil War, 1861-1865—Pictorial works.
I. Künstler, Mort. II. Title.
E468.M229   1992   92-12166
973.7—dc20   CIP

8 7 6 5 4 3 2 1

Acknowledgments

This book would never have come to be if Don Bender, creative director, had not proposed the initial idea and given me encouragement and support throughout the project. J.P. Leventhal, the publisher, and Glorya Hale, editorial director, were invaluable with their advice and made all the important decisions that are necessary in putting together a book of this type. I am indebted to them all for their great patience and expertise.

My sincere appreciation to Professor James McPherson for his magnificent and illuminating text. I am honored by his contribution and can only hope there will be future collaborations.

My sincere thanks to Ted and Mary Sutphen of American Print Gallery, Gettysburg, Pa., for introducing me to the Civil War. I truly believe I have found a "home."

My gratitude to John Heiser and the many other historians with whom I have consulted to ensure accuracy in all these paintings. I am indebted to Richard Lynch, Director of Hammer Galleries, and Howard Shaw and the staff for bringing my paintings to the attention of the art world. Jane Broffman and Paula McEvoy have been invaluable in relieving me of the everyday problems that arise in a busy studio and their efforts are truly appreciated.

And, of course, my heartfelt thanks to my wife, Deborah, who has always done everything possible to help me have the time I need for my second love, painting.

Mort Künstler

CONTENTS

INTRODUCTION
8

AND THE WAR CAME
12

THE REBELS
ARE DESPONDENT
30

A WORSE PLACE
THAN HELL
60

UNVEXED TO THE SEA
90

THE DEEP WATERS
ARE CLOSING OVER US
134

EPILOGUE
170

THE IMAGES
173

INDEX
190

Private Harrison Hunt, 119 Regiment, N.Y.S.V.

INTRODUCTION

THE CIVIL WAR WAS BY FAR the most profound and traumatic experience in American history. The six hundred and twenty thousand soldiers who lost their lives in that conflict almost equaled the number of Americans killed in all the other wars the United States has fought combined. If the same proportion of Americans to the total population were to be killed in a war fought today, the number of American war dead would be *five million.*

No wonder the Civil War made a profound impact on the generation that fought it. And that impact has continued during the century and a quarter since the guns fell silent. More than fifty thousand books and pamphlets about the war have been published. Some of them were best-sellers. An eleven-hour documentary on it presented on public television in 1990 attracted more than fifteen million viewers. At least two hundred Civil War Round Tables meet monthly to discuss a war that seems as much a part of us today as it did to our great-great-grandparents. Several times a year, forty thousand men don woollen uniforms and take up their replica Springfield or Enfield rifles to reenact everything from a minor skirmish in Arizona to the battle of Gettysburg.

It is not only the drama and trauma of the Civil War that have made it so much a part of our national identity that America as we know it is unimaginable without that searing, formative experience. Northern victory in the war also resolved two fundamental, festering problems that had been left unresolved by that other formative experience—the Revolution. First there was the question that preoccupied Americans from 1783 to 1865: Would this fragile experiment in republican government survive in a world bestrode by kings, emperors, czars, and dictators? Most republics throughout history had been overthrown from without or had collapsed from within. Some Americans still alive in 1861 had seen French republics succumb twice to emperors and once to the restoration of the Bourbon monarchy. Republics in Latin America came and went with bewildering rapidity. Would the United States suffer the same fate? Many Americans feared so; many European conservatives hoped so; disunion in 1861 seemed to confirm these fears and fulfill these hopes. As Abraham Lincoln said at Gettysburg in 1863, the Civil War was the great test of whether a republic could endure. The United States passed the test. The Civil War preserved one nation indivisible; since 1865 no state or region has threatened seriously to secede.

The other problem left unresolved by the Revolution was slavery. Founded on a declaration that all people were endowed with the unalienable right of liberty, the United States became the largest slaveholding country in the world, with four million slaves in 1860. As Lincoln put it in 1854: "The monstrous injustice of slavery deprives our republican example of its just influence in the world—enables the enemies of free institutions, with plausibility, to taunt us as hypocrites." Since 1865 that particular injustice and hypocrisy have existed no more.

This book seeks to tell the story of the war, its causes, and its significance in a narrative format that conveys the political and social as well as the military dimensions of the conflict. The narrative tries to present the human as well as the larger impersonal forces of the war. But prose is a limited medium for capturing emotions and passions, the drama of suffering or of triumph, the elation of victory and the despair of defeat, the images of pain or of happiness. To convey these crucial facets of a people at war, one picture is indeed worth a thousand words. That is why artists from Winslow Homer to Mort Künstler have painted the scenes and people of America's bloodiest war. The seventy-two magnificent paintings by Mort Künstler reproduced in this book form the focus of the story for which the words provide a context. Together, words and pictures present an image intended to deepen and enrich the reader's understanding of the most important event of American history.

JAMES M. MCPHERSON

Princeton, New Jersey
1992

VETERANS OF GETTYSBURG

JEFFERSON DAVIS, PRESIDENT OF THE CONFEDERACY

I

AND
THE WAR
CAME

"OF THE AMERICAN CIVIL WAR it may safely be asserted that there was a single cause, slavery." So wrote the foremost Civil War historian of his day, James Ford Rhodes, in 1913. Although historians today would not put it quite so starkly, Rhodes's basic point remains valid.

Other factors suggested as contributors to the war's origins must also be considered. The first half of the nineteenth century witnessed a widening gulf and growing hostility between the South, whose economy was founded on plantation agriculture and the North with its diversifying, industrializing economy. The culture and values of gentry and yeomen in the South increasingly contrasted with the bustling, urbanizing (although still mainly rural) society of the North. At one time, a number of historians denied that these differences generated genuine conflict. Instead, they maintained, self-serving politicians created and then exploited the false issue of slavery's expansion into new territories to whip up these "unimportant" sectional passions and get themselves elected to office. The passions got out of hand and erupted into a needless and avoidable war in 1861.

Today, however, few historians subscribe to this notion of a needless war provoked by self-serving extremists. The war came because of real, profound, intractable problems that Americans on both sides believed went to the heart of their society. These were not merely policy differences between Southern agricultural interests and Northern industry over such issues as tariffs, banks, land grants, and other economic matters. Such differences existed, to be sure. But these issues divided political parties and interest groups more than they did North and South. They have been bread-and-butter issues of American politics before and since the crises of the 1850s over the extension of slavery to new states; indeed, they have generated a good deal more heat on other occasions than they did then. The South in the 1840s and 1850s had its advocates of industrialization and protective tariffs, just as the North had its millions of farmers and its low-tariff, anti-bank Democratic majority in many states. The Civil War was not fought over the issues of a tariff, or industrialization, or land policy. The conflict went much deeper than that.

Nor was it merely a contest over states' rights. Of all the interpretations that have evolved over the years to downplay the centrality of slavery, the states'-rights argument is the flimsiest. It grew up soon after the war when ex-Confederate leaders, trying to salvage as much honor as they could from their recently lost cause, set to work to purge it of any association with the now dead and discredited institution of slavery. Two of the earliest postwar Southern memoirs were written by none other than Confederate ex-President Jefferson Davis and by his vice president, Alexander H. Stephens. Both hewed to the same line: Southern states had seceded not to protect slavery, but to vindicate state sovereignty. This became the virgin-birth theory of secession: the Confederacy was conceived not by any wordly cause, but by constitutional principle. Southern states, Davis insisted, fought solely "for the defense of an inherent, unalienable right . . . to withdraw from a Union into which they had, as sovereign communities, voluntarily entered. . . . The existence of African servitude was in no wise the cause of the conflict, but only an incident." Similarly Alexander Stephens, in a lengthy two-volume memoir entitled *A Constitutional View of the War between the States,* which invented the favorite Southern name for the conflict three years after it was over, declared in his convoluted style that "the War had its origin in *opposing principles*" not concerning slavery, but rather concerning "the organic Structure of the Government of the States. . . . It was a strife between the principles of Federation, on the one side, and Centralism, or Consolidation, on the other."

This was mainly an *ex post facto* rationalization. Neither Davis nor Stephens had spoken that way in 1861, when slavery flourished and most Southern whites believed it to be divinely ordained as a necessary and desirable order of society. Then Jefferson Davis, a large slaveholder, justified secession as an act of self-defense against the new Republican administration of Abraham Lincoln, whose policy of excluding slavery from the territories would make "property in slaves so insecure as to be comparatively worthless . . . thereby annihilating in effect property worth thousands of millions of dollars." And in a famous speech at Savannah on March 21, 1861, Stephens said that slavery was "the immediate cause of the late rupture and the present revolution" of Confederate independence. The old confederation called the United States, Stephens said, had been founded on the false idea that all men are created equal. The new Confederacy, by contrast, "is founded upon exactly the opposite ideas; its foundations are laid, its cornerstone rests, upon the great truth that the negro is not equal to the white man; that slavery, subordination to the superior race, is his natural and moral condition. This, our new Government, is the first, in the history of the world, based on this great physical, philosophical, and moral truth."

No talk of states' rights here. So long as the South controlled the national government, as it did most of the time before 1861, Southerners were quite content to rely on this power to protect slavery. It was when they lost control of the national government that they invoked state sovereignty and went out of the Union. The strongest exercise of national power before 1861 was carried out by Southerners in defense of slavery. This was the Fugitive Slave Law, passed mainly by Southern votes in Congress as part of the Compromise of 1850. This law overrode the legislatures and officials of Northern states and extended the long arm of national law, enforced by the army and navy, into Northern cities to recover escaped slaves and return them to their owners. When Northern state legislatures and courts invoked states' rights and individual liberties against this federal law, the United States Supreme Court, with its majority of Southern justices, rode roughshod over the Northern states and reaffirmed the supremacy of national law to protect slavery. It was the South's loss of this national power brought about by Lincoln's election, and not the principle of states' rights, that impelled secession.

Slavery had existed in all the British colonies that united in 1776 to declare their independence. But the libertarian philosophy of the American Revolution, combined with the economic marginality of slavery in the states north of the Mason-Dixon line, produced its abolition in those states. At the same time, the invention in 1793 of the cotton gin, which made the growing of short-staple cotton profitable, gave slavery in the

SOJOURNER TRUTH

South a new and powerful lease on life. In subsequent decades the cotton kingdom marched westward from the Carolinas to Texas, doubling the harvest of this white gold every decade until the American South produced three-quarters of the world's cotton. And almost nine-tenths of that American cotton was grown by slaves. These slaves were the most valuable form of property in the South; their market value of three billion dollars in 1860 was equivalent, as a proportion of national wealth, to three trillion dollars in the United States of 1992. Little wonder that in 1861 Jefferson Davis embraced secession as the best means to protect this huge economic stake from the threat posed by the election of an antislavery president of the United States.

As the northern states abolished slavery and their economy developed agricultural, commercial, and industrial sectors based on free labor, movements arose in the North to condemn slavery as economically regressive, morally evil, and an ugly stain on the much-boasted American ideal of liberty. The most militant version of abolitionism branded slaveholding a sin and called on Americans immediately to expiate that sin by freeing all slaves. The principal founder and leader of militant abolitionism was William Lloyd Garrison. His inaugural editorial in 1831 in his newspaper *The Liberator* set the tone for this crusade against human bondage: "I will be as harsh as truth, and as uncompromising as justice. On this subject, I do not wish to think, or speak, or write, with moderation. . . . I am in earnest—I will not equivocate—I will not excuse—I will not retreat a single inch—AND I WILL BE HEARD."

Some of Garrison's earliest supporters were free blacks including former slaves like Frederick Douglass, whose eloquence took on added force because he could testify personally to the evils of slavery. Abolitionism also spawned the women's rights movement in America. Women who spoke out against the slave's subordination to the master became sensitized to their own subordination to men. In 1848, numerous female and a few male abolitionists met in a church in Seneca Falls, New York, to hold the world's first women's rights convention.

A frequent speaker at women's rights as well as abolitionist meetings was Sojourner Truth, born a slave named Isabella who had seen two of her children sold away from her before she gained legal freedom in 1827. A religious mystic, she had taken the name Sojourner Truth in 1843 because she traveled through the North preaching the truth of racial and sexual equality. Her oratory was colloquial but powerful; one might "as well attempt to report the seven apocalyptic thunders" as to describe it, wrote one abolitionist. Truth's most famous speech was delivered at a women's rights convention in 1851 at Akron, Ohio, where hecklers jeered the speakers and cheered a man who shouted that women did not deserve equality because they were weak and helpless. Sojourner Truth leaped to the stage, silenced the hecklers, and electrified the crowd with these words: "The man over there says women need to be helped into carriages and lifted over ditches, and to have the best place everywhere. Nobody ever helps me into carriages or over puddles, or gives me the best place— and ain't I a woman?" Baring her right arm, she continued, "Look at my arm! I have ploughed and planted and gathered into barns, and no man could head me—and ain't I a woman? I could work as much and eat as much as a man—when I could get it—and bear the lash as well! And ain't

I a woman? I have borne thirteen children [an exaggeration], and seen most of 'em sold into slavery, and when I cried out with my mother's grief, none but Jesus heard me—and ain't I a woman?''

Reformers like Garrison and Truth caused white Southerners to shudder not only because they challenged two of the South's fundamental institutions, slavery and patriarchy, but also because they represented the ferment of radicalism that swept through the North in those years. Southerners—and Northern conservatives—loathed and feared these isms, not only abolitionism and feminism but a host of others including utopianism, millenarianism, socialism, and transcendentalism. Slavery insulated the South from such isms, boasted Southern leaders, for "the bondsmen, as a lower class, as the substratum of society, constitute an always-reliable, never-wavering foundation whereon the social fabric rests securely, rooted and grounded in stability, and entirely beyond the reach of agitation."

This conviction formed an essential part of the "positive good" defense of slavery that emerged after 1830 as a response to abolitionist condemnation of it as an evil. Many Southern whites had once shared Thomas Jefferson's conviction that bondage was an evil—albeit a "necessary evil." They hoped that slavery would eventually disappear—in God's own good time. But as they came under abolitionist attack, and as they contemplated the economic and social costs of emancipation, Southern whites circled the wagons and defended slavery as a "positive good," a social order ordained by God for the benefit of both races and the stability of a biracial society. "Many in the South once believed that slavery was a moral and political evil," said John C. Calhoun, the foremost Southern spokesman, in 1838. "That folly and delusion are gone. We see it now in its true light, and regard it as the most safe and stable basis for free institutions in the world."

Though genuine abolitionsts were a minority in the North, by the 1840s most Yankees considered slavery wrong in some degree. The institution of bondage defined the growing gulf between North and South. The two largest Protestant denominations, Methodists and Baptists, split into separate Northern and Southern churches in the 1840s over the issue of slavery. Other national organizations also divided along sectional lines. Although they shared a common cultural and political heritage, many Northerners and many Southerners came to see themselves as separate peoples. As a lawyer in Savannah, Georgia, expressed it in 1860, "in this country have arisen two races [i.e., Yankee and 'Southron'] which, although claiming a common parentage, have been so entirely separated by climate, by morals, by religion, and by estimates so totally opposite to all that constitutes honor, truth, and manliness, that they cannot longer exist under the same government." What had caused this separation? Slavery. It was the sole institution not shared by North and South. Both had cities, farms, railroads, ports, factories, colleges, poets, poverty, wealth, slums, mansions, capitalists, workers, immigrants, ethnic and class conflict, and almost everything else that might be named—but only one had slavery. "On the subject of slavery," declared the *Charleston Mercury* in 1858, "the North and South . . . are not only two Peoples, but they are rival, hostile Peoples."

Two of the North's foremost political leaders echoed this point in the same year—1858. Slavery and freedom, said Senator William H. Seward of New York, who expected to be the Republican presidential nominee in 1860, are "more than incongruous—they are incompatible." The collision between them "is an irrepressible conflict between opposing and enduring forces, and it means that the United States must and will, sooner or later, become either entirely a slaveholding nation, or entirely a free-labor nation." In his famous "House Divided" speech, which launched his campaign for the Senate in 1858, Abraham Lincoln—who lost that election but did become the Republican presidential nominee in 1860—declared that " 'a house divided against itself cannot stand.' I believe this government cannot endure permanently half slave and half free."

It was not only the cultural and ideological conflict over slavery, but more important, the political contest over its expansion into the territories that brought the issue to a crisis in 1860. The annexation of Texas in 1845 had added a new slave state, and the conquest of the Southwest in the Mexican War created the potential for several more. The Compromise of 1850 temporarily papered over the rift, but events in the 1850s opened it wider than ever. Senator Stephen A. Douglas of Illinois had maneuvered the Compromise of 1850 through Congress. Its key provision was "popular sovereignty"—leaving it to the people in the territories to choose for or against slavery. In 1854 Douglas tried to apply the same principle to the Kansas and Nebraska territories. But this meant repealing the provisions of the Missouri Compromise of 1820 that had banned slavery from these territories. Southern domination of the Democratic party had forced Douglas to take this step.

Bloody fighting between proslavery and antislavery settlers in the Kansas territory added bullets to ballots in the contest over slavery's expansion. Capitalizing on Northern fears of the "Slave Power," the new-born Republican party ran its first presidential candidate in 1856 on a platform of keeping slavery out of the territories, and carried most Northern states. Confirming the worst Northern fears, the Southern-dominated Supreme Court in the Dred Scott decision of 1857 proclaimed the legality of slavery in all territories on grounds that seemed to permit slaveowners to take their human property into free states as well.

This was the setting in which Abraham Lincoln ran against Stephen Douglas for the Senate in 1858 and challenged him to a series of debates. The debates in seven towns throughout Illinois became justly famous. Their sole topic was slavery and its effect on the future of the United States. The old staples of American politics—the tariff, banks, public works, public land policy, and the like—were conspicuous by their absence. Lincoln maintained that the obsolete and immoral institution of slavery must eventually disappear if the country took seriously the ideals of freedom on which it was founded. By preventing slavery's further expansion, Lincoln hoped to put the institution "in the course of ultimate extinction."

Douglas charged that Lincoln's policy would destroy the Union by driving the South to secession. Let the people of Kansas, or Nebraska, or New Mexico, or any new territory such as Cuba (which had slavery) that might be annexed decide for themselves whether to have slavery, said Douglas. He professed himself no friend of slavery—he did not want it in Illinois—but he cared not whether they voted it up or down in Kansas. By the Dred Scott decision, which Douglas endorsed, slavery was legal in Kansas, but he believed it could not flourish there unless the majority wanted it—and if they did, they should have it.

Lincoln deplored this "care not" attitude. Douglas *"looks to no end of the institution of slavery,"* said Lincoln. Indeed, by endorsing the Dred Scott decision he looks to its *"perpetuity and nationalization."* That was the real issue, insisted Lincoln.

> That is the issue that will continue in this country when these poor tongues of Judge Douglas and myself are silent. It is the eternal struggle between these two principles—right and wrong— throughout the world. The one is the common right of humanity and the other the divine right of kings. No matter in what shape it comes, whether from a king who seeks to bestride the people of his own nation and live by the fruit of their labor, or from one race of men as an apology for enslaving another race, it is the same tyrannical principle.

Douglas narrowly won reelection to the Senate. But Lincoln won national recognition in the debates that laid the groundwork for his nomination to the presidency in 1860. And Douglas got into trouble with the Southern wing of his own party for not defending slavery vigorously enough. In 1859 the Southern Democrats led by Jefferson Davis insisted on a policy of federal military protection for slavery in the territories. When Douglas refused to go along with this—because it would destroy the Democratic party in the North—Southern delegates walked out of the 1860 Democratic national convention, formed a new "Southern Rights" Democratic party, and nominated their own candidate. One of the most incandescent of Southern Rights fire-eaters was Congressman William Barksdale of Mississippi, who fiercely favored secession and thirsted for military glory in the war he expected to come. (He would get his wish, killed at Gettysburg leading his Mississippi brigade.)

The indignation which Abraham Lincoln felt about the Dred Scott decision led him back to politics in 1857. In the legendary series of debates for the Senate seat from Illinois, Lincoln was pitted against Stephen A. Douglas, known as "the little giant" because of his prodigious speechmaking ability. Their first encounter (right) took place at Ottawa on August 21, 1858. Lincoln, at 6 feet 4 inches, was more than a foot taller than Douglas. While the fiery, animated Douglas stirred his listeners, Lincoln spoke directly to the hearts and minds of the people with the voice of the common man. Although Douglas prevailed and won the election, Lincoln gained the national recognition that eventually led to the presidency.

It was this split in the Democratic party and the preference of a majority of Northern voters for the Republican position of excluding slavery from the territories that gave Lincoln the presidency with the electoral votes of every Northern state (and no Southern state). Regarding this as an insult as well as an injury, the seven Deep-South states seceded one after another, beginning with South Carolina on December 20, 1860, and continuing through Texas on February 1, 1861. All efforts at compromise to stop the hemorrhage and stitch together the Union proved unavailing. No compromise, no assurance by Lincoln that he had no intention of interfering with slavery in the states where it existed could undo the fact of his election entirely by Northern votes on a slavery-restriction platform. For Southerners this was the handwriting on the wall. They had lost control of the national government to the "Black Republicans." This meant loss of control over their future in the Union. So they departed the Union, asserting their right to do so on grounds of state sovereignty.

But none of these seven states could stand alone. They called a convention to meet at Montgomery, Alabama, on February 4, 1861, to form a new confederation of slave states, hoping that some of the other eight would join them. To project a moderate image, the convention adopted a Confederate Constitution modeled on the familiar United States Constitution, with additional clauses to protect slavery and to strengthen states' rights. As president of the new Confederacy, the convention elected Jefferson Davis, one of the most respected and experienced political leaders of the South. Davis was a West Point graduate and a Mexican War veteran who had also served as secretary of war for four years—useful qualifications if the new nation had to fight for its survival. For vice president, the delegates chose Alexander H. Stephens, who had actually opposed secession until his state of Georgia voted for it. With this conservative image, Confederate leaders appealed to the Upper-South states still clinging to the old Union to join the new one on grounds of the "common origin, pursuits, tastes, manners and customs" that "bind together in one brotherhood the slaveholding states."

With a heavy heart, Jefferson Davis left his plantation in Mississippi to take up his new burden as Confederate president. He would have preferred command of the Confederate army to the refractory problems of statecraft in a new nation dwarfed in population and resources by the old one it had left.

Davis arrived in Montgomery on February 16 and was introduced to the crowd by William L. Yancey, Alabama's firebrand of secession, with the ringing words: "The man and the hour have met!" Inspired by these words, and perhaps also by the playing of "Dixie," which began its career here as the unofficial Confederate anthem, Davis made a brief, bellicose speech. "The time for compromise is now passed," he told the cheering crowd. "The South is determined to maintain her position, and make all who oppose her smell Southern powder and feel Southern steel." Upon reflection, however, he softened his tone considerably in the formal inaugural address two days later. Beneath a bright sun on the steps of the colonnaded state Capitol, Davis reaffirmed an inflexible determination to maintain Confederate independence, but he also insisted that the new nation wished to live in peace and extended a warm welcome to any states that "may seek to unite their fortunes to ours."

GENERAL WILLIAM BARKSDALE, MISSISSIPPI

Two weeks later, in his inaugural address Abraham Lincoln also spoke of peace and appealed to the latent American nationalism of Southerners. "We must not be enemies," said Lincoln. "Though passion may have strained, it must not break our bonds of affection. The mystic chords of memory, stretching from every battlefield, and patriot grave, to every living heart and hearthstone, all over this broad land, will yet swell the chorus of the Union, when again touched, as surely they will be, by the better angels of our nature."

Was war inevitable? In hindsight it appears so. Lincoln's insistence on maintaining the Union was as firm as Davis's insistence on separation. Lincoln was not willing to "let the erring sisters depart in peace." To accept disunion would set a fatal precedent whereby a disaffected minority could leave the Union whenever it lost a presidential election. The United States would cease to exist, becoming like Central or South America, with a dozen or more squabbling autocracies. The great experiment in republican self-government by majority rule launched in 1776 would collapse, proving the contention of European conservatives and monarchists that this upstart republic across the Atlantic could not last. "The central idea pervading this struggle," said Lincoln in 1861, "is the necessity that is upon us, of proving that popular government is not an absurdity. We must settle this question now, whether in a free government the minority have the right to break up the government whenever they choose. If we fail it will go far to prove the incapability of the people to govern themselves."

The 1861 call to arms was a challenge to defend the homeland, and thousands of men and boys thronged into recruiting offices. From Arkansas to Florida, Southerners enlisted to learn a new trade and defend their home states, the flags of which they first carried off to war. Peaceful farmers, like this young Floridian, were suddenly soldiers.

So saying, Lincoln nevertheless did not consider war inevitable when he took office. If he could keep the other eight slave states in the Union, he hoped the hot passions of the winter of 1860–1861 would cool, and the good sense and residual nationalism of people even in the Deep South would bring them back. It was a vain hope. The sticking point was Fort Sumter, a large fortress in Charleston harbor built to protect the city from foreign attack. As Southern states had seceded, they had seized United States property within their borders—arsenals, mints, forts, and custom-houses. But Fort Sumter, a mile or more from land in the middle of Charleston Bay, defended by eighty-odd soldiers commanded by Major Robert Anderson of Kentucky, could not be seized without a fight.

Lincoln came under pressure from conservatives and Upper-South Unionists to yield the fort as a gesture of peace and goodwill that might strengthen Southern Unionism. After leaning in this direction for a time, Lincoln concluded that to give up Sumter would achieve the opposite: It would demoralize Unionists and strengthen the Confederacy. Fort Sumter had become a master symbol of sovereignty. To yield it would consti-tute *de facto* recognition of Confederate sovereignty. It would surely en-courage European nations to grant diplomatic recognition to the Confederate nation. It would make a mockery of Lincoln's inaugural pledge to "hold, occupy, and possess" national property in the states.

So Lincoln devised an ingenious plan to put the burden of decision for war or peace on Jefferson Davis's shoulders. In April 1861, the garrison at Fort Sumter was about to run out of provisions. Giving advance notice of his intentions, Lincoln sent a fleet toward Charleston with supplies and reinforcements. If the Confederates allowed the unarmed boats to bring in "food for hungry men," the warships would stand off and the reinforce-ments would return north. But if they fired on the fleet, the ships and the fort would fire back. In effect, Lincoln flipped a coin and told Jefferson Davis: "Heads I win; tails you lose." If Confederate guns fired first, the South would stand convicted of starting a war. If they let the supplies go in, the American flag would continue to fly over Fort Sumter. The Con-federacy would lose face; Southern Unionists would take courage.

Davis did not hesitate. He considered it vital to assert the Confeder-acy's sovereignty. He also hoped that the outbreak of a shooting war would force the Upper South to join their sister slave states. Davis or-dered General Pierre G. T. Beauregard, commander of Confederate troops at Charleston, to open fire on Fort Sumter before the supply ships got there. At 4:30 A.M. on April 12, Confederate artillery started the Civil War by firing on Fort Sumter. After a thirty-three-hour bombardment in which the Confederates fired four thousand rounds and the skeleton crews in the fort replied with a thousand—killing no one on either side in the first clash of this bloodiest of wars—the burning fort lowered the American flag in surrender. As Lincoln put it four years later in his second inaugural address: "Both [sides] deprecated war; but one of them would *make* war rather than let the nation survive; and the other would *accept* war rather than let it perish. And the war came."

GENERAL PIERRE G. T. BEAUREGARD, LOUISIANA

Fort Sumter lay at the mouth of Charleston Harbor and was "invariably the sorest thumb in one's side," as South Carolina newspapermen considered it. Confederate authorities were more concerned that the Union-held fort was a test of their will and an invasion of their declared sovereignty. A little after 4:30 A.M. on April 12, Confederate batteries that ringed the harbor opened fire while Charleston's populace crowded rooftops to watch the spectacle. The fort's commander, Major Robert Anderson, ordered the guns within the fort to be manned, abandoning the cannon on the top of the fort. At one point during the bombardment, Sergeant John Carmody ran to the upper parapet and fired the previously loaded guns. But his solitary act of defiance and bravery was not enough to prevent the surrender of Fort Sumter and the onset of the American Civil War.

II

THE
REBELS
ARE
DESPONDENT

GENERAL ROBERT E. LEE

THE ATTACK ON FORT SUMTER galvanized the North. "The town is in a wild state of excitement," wrote a Philadelphia diarist. "The American flag is to be seen everywhere. Men are enlisting as fast as possible." A New York woman wrote that the "time before Sumter" seemed like another century. "It seems as if we were never alive till now; never had a country till now."

The tiny United States Army of sixteen thousand men, most of them stationed at remote frontier posts, was inadequate for the crisis—especially since nearly one-third of its officers were resigning to go with the Confederacy. So Lincoln called on the loyal states for seventy-five thousand militia to suppress the insurrection. The free states filled their quotas immediately. More than double the number called volunteered. Recognizing that the ninety days' service to which the militia were limited by law would be too short a time, on May 3 Lincoln issued a call for three-year volunteers. Even before the shooting had started at Fort Sumter, the Confederate Congress had authorized an army of one hundred thousand men. Through the summer of 1861 both sides multiplied their calls for troops. By the time the war was over, more than three million men had served in the armed forces—2,200,000 for the Union, 900,000 for the Confederacy.

Lincoln's initial call for militia forced the eight slave states that were still in the Union to make a choice. Four of them—Virginia, Arkansas, Tennessee, and North Carolina—soon seceded and joined the Confederacy "for the defense of our rights and those of our Southern brothers," as the governor of Tennessee put it. A North Carolinian who had remained on the fence until Lincoln's call for troops expressed the reason for his choice: "The division must be made on the line of slavery. The South must go with the South. Blood is thicker than water."

No man found this choice harder to make than Robert E. Lee of Virginia. One of the most promising officers in the United States Army, Lee did not believe in the legal right of secession. But when Virginia's convention passed an ordinance of secession on April 17, with great sadness Lee resigned from the army in which he had spent his whole career. "I must side either with or against my section," Lee told a Northern friend. "I cannot raise my hand against my birthplace, my home, my children." Along with three sons and a nephew, Lee joined the Confederate Army. "I foresee that the country will have to pass through a terrible ordeal," he wrote, "a necessary expiation perhaps for our national sins."

But most Southerners felt a great deal less foreboding and more enthusiasm than Lee. When news of Fort Sumter's surrender reached Richmond, a huge crowd poured into the state capital square and ran up a Confederate flag. "Everyone is in favor of secession" and "perfectly frantic with delight," wrote a participant. "I never in my life witnessed such excitement." A London *Times* correspondent described crowds in North Carolina with "flushed faces, wild eyes, screaming mouths, hurrahing for 'Jeff Davis' and 'the Southern Confederacy.'" No one in these cheering crowds could know that, before the war ended, at least two hundred and sixty thousand Confederate soldiers would lose their lives (along with

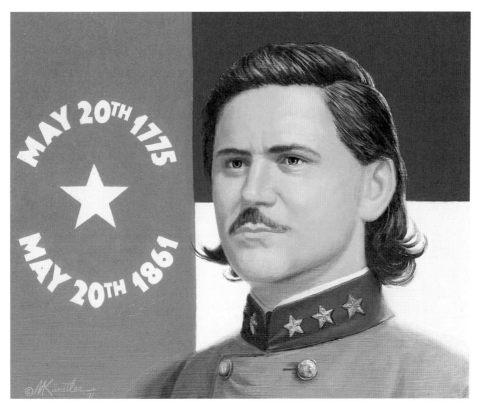

COLONEL ZEBULON B. VANCE, NORTH CAROLINA

three hundred and sixty thousand Union soldiers) and that the South they fought to defend would be utterly destroyed.

The slave states that bordered free states were badly divided by the outbreak of war. Little Delaware, however, remained firmly in the Union. The governor of Maryland was a Unionist, but many members of the legislature were not. The governors of Kentucky and Missouri favored the Confederacy, but a majority of their constituents were Unionists. Leaders in all three states spoke vaguely of "neutrality" but were to be denied that luxury. Kentucky's strategic importance was so great—with a four-hundred-mile frontier between North and South, the Ohio and Mississippi rivers flowing along its borders, and the Tennessee and Cumberland rivers flowing through it from the heart of the Confederacy—that it was only a matter of time until armies and gunboats of both sides penetrated the state. The time came in September 1861, making Kentucky a battle-ground for field armies during part of the war and guerrilla and cavalry raids during all of it. But Union forces maintained a shaky political control of the state.

The same was true of Missouri, which was wracked by more vicious guerrilla conflict than any other region. Confederate "bushwhackers" and Unionist "jayhawkers" turned large parts of the state into a no-man's-land of hit-and-run raids, ambushes, arson, and murder. The famous post-war outlaws Jesse and Frank James and Cole and Jim Younger rode with the notorious rebel guerrilla chieftains William Quantrill and "Bloody Bill" Anderson, who liked to festoon his horse with the scalps of Union-ists he had killed. The bitter legacy of Missouri's civil war within the Civil War, which dated back to the proslavery raids into Kansas territory during the 1850s, persisted for generations after 1865.

Aggressive action at the outset of the conflict set the stage for the tone of war in Missouri. Union troops commanded by fiery, red-haired Nathaniel Lyon surrounded and captured a camp of pro-Confederate militia in St. Louis on May 10. While marching the captives through the city, the troops were fired on by a mob. They fired back, provoking a bloodbath in which at least three dozen people were killed. Following up his advantage, Lyon defeated the Confederates in skirmishes along the Missouri River, in which the only bright spot for the rebels was the leadership shown by a young officer, John Sappington Marmaduke, scion of a talented cavalry commander in the trans-Mississippi theater. During the summer Lyon drove the Confederate Missourians to the extreme southwest corner of the state. But there the rebels received reinforcements from Arkansas and turned on Lyon's outnumbered force. On August 10, a fierce battle along the rolling prairie bordering Wilson's Creek ten miles south of Springfield, Missouri, resulted in the death of Lyon, a bullet through his heart, and the retreat of Union troops. The victorious Confederates marched northward all the way to the Missouri River, where they captured a Union garrison at Lexington forty miles east of Kansas City on September 20. By then, however, Union forces had regrouped; by the end of 1861 they once again drove the ragged Confederates into Arkansas. Unionists thereafter remained in control of the state, but not without harassment by guerrillas that tied down many thousands of Northern troops.

The battle of Wilson's Creek was, next to Bull Run, the bloodiest during the first year of war. The proportion of casualties suffered by both sides at Wilson's Creek was higher than those in the larger armies at Bull Run. But Missouri was more than a thousand miles from the Union and Confederate capitals. The "media" of the day paid a great deal more attention to events in the eastern theater—and history has tended to follow suit. Events in the east were dramatic enough, starting on April 19 with a clash between a Baltimore secession mob and a regiment of Massachusetts soldiers on their way to defend Washington that left twelve Baltimoreans and four soldiers dead on the street. The stakes in Maryland were high, for if it joined the Confederacy the United States capital would be surrounded by enemy territory. Following the clash in Baltimore, Northern troops occupied the city and other parts of the state. They arrested numerous Confederate sympathizers, including the mayor and police chief of Baltimore, a judge, and two dozen state legislators. This reinforced the Unionism of the majority of Marylanders and kept the state safe for the Union.

Northern troops helped to create a fifth Union border state during the war itself: West Virginia. Most of the delegates to Virginia's convention in 1861 who were from the part of the state west of the Shenandoah Valley voted against secession. The economy of this mountainous region of small farms and few slaves was linked more closely to nearby Ohio and Pennsylvania than to the South. Its largest city, Wheeling, was three hundred and thirty miles from Richmond, but only sixty miles from Pittsburgh. A majority of political leaders there, having opposed Virginia's secession from the Union, determined to carry out western Virginia's secession from Virginia. Troops from Ohio and Indiana crossed the Ohio River at the end of May 1861 to help them. Their commander was

GENERAL JOHN SAPPINGTON MARMADUKE, MISSOURI

George B. McClellan, a railroad president and West Point graduate who launched his meteoric but star-crossed Civil War career by winning several small battles during June and July. This enabled local Unionists, through a complicated process of conventions and referendums, to create in 1862 the new state of West Virginia, which entered the Union in 1863.

The struggle for the border states was the main activity in the first summer of the war. During those months of 1861, both sides also mobilized the largest armies in American history up to that time. These men were volunteers from civilian life who rushed to the colors to support the competing versions of American and Confederate nationalism. They were impatient to get through the drill and training they received, superficial though it was, and eager to see action. (That would change after they actually experienced combat.)

Union General-in-Chief Winfield Scott, a seventy-five-year-old veteran of the War of 1812 and the Mexican War, in which he had commanded the forces that captured Mexico City, was reluctant to commit his raw ninety-day militia to action in 1861. A native of Virginia who hoped the Union could be preserved without destroying his native section, Scott developed a military strategy founded on a belief that a large pool of potential Unionism still existed in the South. The main elements of his strategy were a naval blockade and a combined army-navy expedition down the Mississippi to gain control of that river, thus sealing off the Confederates from the world with a cordon on all sides, enabling the government to "bring them to terms with less bloodshed than by any other plan."

The battle of Wilson's Creek had raged for several hours on August 10, 1861, and the Third Louisiana had seen their fair share of combat. Suddenly taken from the main line of battle and marched to the left, the gray-clad Southerners strained to see what their next task would be. "Come on my brave lads," General Ben McCulloh shouted to them. "I have a battery for you to charge and the day is ours!" Without hesitation, the Louisiana infantrymen, led by Colonel James McIntosh, rushed upon the lone Union battery, scattering the gunners and chasing away most of the Union infantry. Remarkably, it was the turning point of the battle, and a significant blow to Union strategy in Missouri.

The Northern press gently ridiculed Scott's strategy as "the Anaconda Plan," after the South American snake that squeezed its victims to death. Most Northerners believed that resistance could be overcome only by victory in battle. Virginia became the main potential battleground, especially after the Confederate government moved its capital to Richmond in May 1861. "FORWARD TO RICHMOND," clamored Northern newspapers. And forward toward Richmond moved a Union army of thirty-five thousand men in July 1861, despite the misgivings of Scott and of Irvin McDowell, the army's field commander. Both felt that these green troops were not ready to fight a real battle. They got no farther than Bull Run, a sluggish stream twenty-five miles southwest of Washington, where a Confederate army commanded by Beauregard, the "hero of Fort Sumter," was deployed to defend a key rail junction at Manassas.

Another small Confederate army in the Shenandoah Valley under General Joseph E. Johnston had given a Union force the slip and traveled to Manassas by rail to reinforce Beauregard. On July 21 the attacking Federals forded Bull Run and hit the Confederates on the left flank, driving them back and appearing to be on the verge of a victory by early afternoon. But a Virginia brigade commanded by Thomas J. Jackson stood "like a stone wall," giving Jackson the nickname he carried ever after. By midafternoon Confederate reinforcements—including one brigade just off the train from the Shenandoah Valley—had grouped for a screaming counterattack. (The famed "rebel yell" was first heard here.) They drove the exhausted and disorganized Yankees back across Bull Run in a retreat that became a rout.

Although the battle of Manassas (or Bull Run, as Northerners called it) was a small battle by later Civil War standards, it made a profound impression on both sides. Of the eighteen thousand men actually engaged on each side, Union casualties (killed, wounded, and captured) were about two thousand eight hundred and Confederate casualties two thousand. The victory exhilarated Southerners and confirmed their image of themselves as better soldiers than the Yankees. It instilled a morale advantage in Confederate forces in the Virginia theater that persisted for two years. At the same time, however, Manassas bred overconfidence in the Confederacy. Some Southerners thought the war was over. Northerners, by contrast, were jolted out of their expectations of a short war. A new mood of reality and grim determination gripped the North. Congress authorized the enlistment of up to a million three-year volunteers. In the next few months hundreds of thousands of men flocked to recruiting offices. Lincoln called George B. McClellan from western Virginia to Washington to organize these new troops into the Army of the Potomac.

An energetic, talented officer, only thirty-four years old, small in stature but great with an aura of destiny, McClellan soon won the sobriquet of "The Young Napoleon" from his admirers. In Washington he took hold with a firm grasp during those summer and fall months of 1861. He organized and trained the Army of the Potomac into a large, well-disciplined and well-equipped fighting force. He was just what the North needed after its dispiriting defeat at Bull Run. When the aging Scott, suffering from dropsy and vertigo and unable to mount a horse, stepped down as general-in-chief on November 1, McClellan took his place.

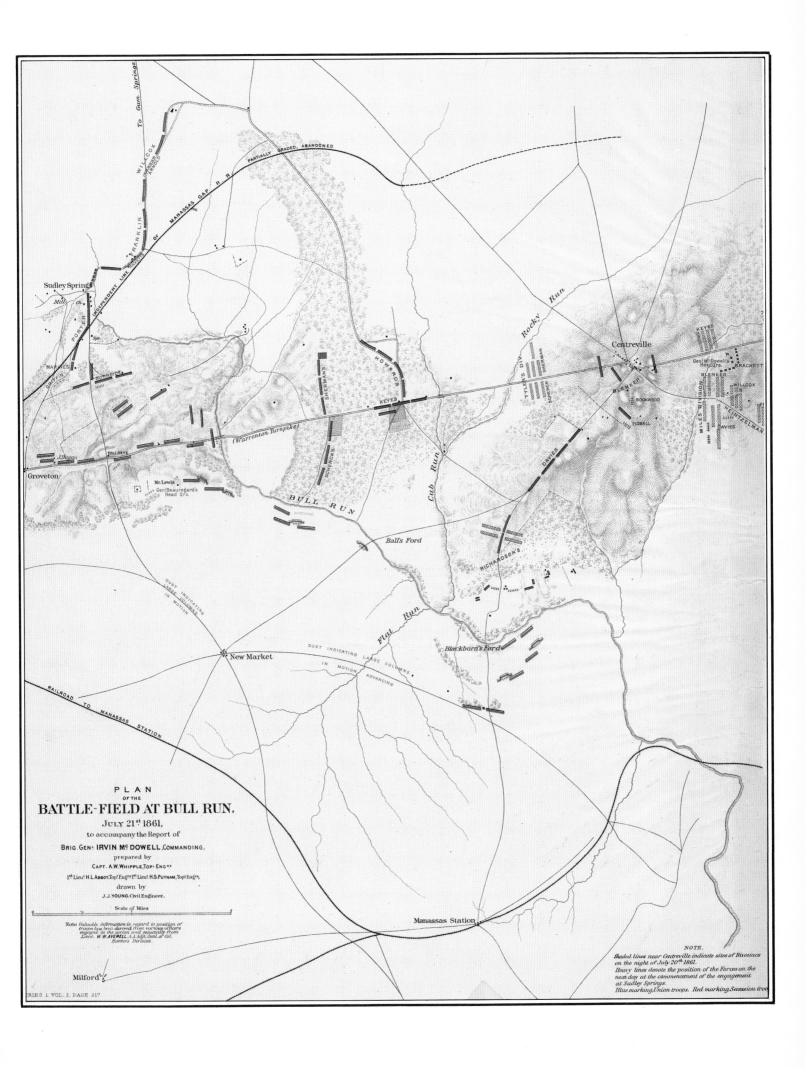

PLAN
OF THE
BATTLE-FIELD AT BULL RUN,
JULY 21ˢᵗ 1861,
to accompany the Report of
BRIG. GENˡ IRVIN McDOWELL, COMMANDING,
prepared by
CAPT. A. W. WHIPPLE, Topˡ Engˢ,
1ˢᵗ Lieuᵗ H. L. ABBOT, Topˡ Engˢ 1ˢᵗ Lieuᵗ H. S. PUTNAM, Topˡ Engˢ,
drawn by
J. J. YOUNG, Civil Engineer.

Scale of Miles

Note *Valuable information in regard to position of
troops has been derived from various officers
engaged in the action and especially from
Lieut. W. W. AVERELL, A.A.Adjt. Genl. & Col.
Hunter's Division.*

NOTE.
*Shaded lines near Centreville indicate sites of Bivouacs
on the night of July 20ᵗʰ 1861.
Heavy lines denote the position of the Forces on the
next day at the commencement of the engagement
at Sudley Springs.
Blue marking, Union troops. Red marking, Secession troo[ps]*

Sudley Springs
Mill Ch.
Spr.
MARINES
GRIFFIN
BURNSIDE
PORTER INDEPENDENT LINE
FRANKLIN Or MANASSAS GAP R. R.
PARTIALLY GRADED, ABANDONED
To Gum. Springs
WILLCOX
ARNOLD
J. Hogan
TOLL GATE
Groveton
Mr. Lewis
Genˡ Beauregard's Head Qrs.
(Warrenton Turnpike)
SHERMANS
HOWARDS
KEYES
SCHENCKS
BULL RUN
Ball's Ford
DUST INDICATING
LARGE COLUMNS
IN MOTION
New Market
Flat Run
DUST INDICATING LARGE COLUMNS
IN MOTION ADVANCING
RAILROAD TO MANASSAS STATION
Cub Run
Rocky Run
TYLER'S DIV.
SHERMAN
SCHENCK
DAVIES
Centreville
Genˡ McDowell's Head Qrs.
BLENKER
ROCKWOOD
TIDBALL
KEYES
BRACKETT
BLENKER
WILLCOX
MILES DIVISION
HEINTZELMAN
DAVIES
RICHARDSON'S
Blackburn's Ford
Manassas Station
Milford

RIES I. VOL. 2. PAGE 317

On July 21, 1861 the attacking Union forces forded Bull Run and hit the Confederates on the left flank. They drove them back and, by early afternoon, appeared to be on the verge of a victory. But a Virginia brigade commanded by Thomas J. Jackson stood "like a stone wall," giving Jackson the nickname he carried ever after. By mid-afternoon Confederate reinforcements—including one brigade just off the train from the Shenandoah Valley—had grouped for a screaming counterattack and drove the exhausted and disorganized Yankees back across Bull Run.

The Confederates won through perseverance, luck, and the determination of Jackson, an unassuming, pious VMI professor. Perhaps the legend that grew about him was the most important legacy to come from the first battle of Bull Run. Here was born a symbol for the Confederacy and for southern generations for years to come; the legacy that was "Stonewall" Jackson.

But as winter approached and McClellan did nothing to advance against the smaller Confederate army, whose outposts stood only a few miles from Washington, his faults as a commander began to become evident. He was a perfectionist in a profession where nothing could ever be perfect. His army was perpetually *almost* ready to begin active operations. McClellan was afraid to take risks; he never learned the military lesson that no victory can be won without risking defeat. He consistently overestimated the strength of enemy forces facing him (sometimes by a factor of two or three) and used these estimates as a reason for inaction until he could increase his own forces.

When criticism of McClellan began to appear in the press and among Republicans in Congress (McClellan was a Democrat), he grew defensive and accused his critics of political motives. Having built a fine fighting machine, he was afraid to start it up for fear it might break. The caution and defensiveness that McClellan instilled in the Army of the Potomac's officer corps persisted for more than a year after Lincoln eventually removed him from command in November 1862.

Because of McClellan, after the battle of Manassas little action occurred in the Virginia theater until the spring of 1862. The Union Navy took over the spotlight for several months. The navy's main task was a blockade of Confederate ports, a crucial element in Union strategy. As an agricultural society, the South depended on imports for most of its manufactured goods. This need became doubly acute in wartime. Although Josiah Gorgas, the Confederate ordnance chief, accomplished near-miracles in the establishment of gunpowder and munitions factories during the war, the Confederacy could not survive without imports of ordnance and a wide variety of war materiel and industrial products, or without exports of cotton to pay for them.

Lincoln therefore proclaimed a blockade on April 19, 1861. At first this was more a policy than a reality, for the navy had only a few ships immediately available to enforce it. The task was formidable, because the Confederate coastline stretched for thirty-five hundred miles with two dozen major ports and another hundred and fifty bays or coves where cargo could be landed. The U.S. Navy, which since the 1840s had been converting from sail to steam, called its ships home from distant seas, took old sailing vessels out of mothballs, and bought or chartered suitable merchant ships and armed them in an attempt to create an overnight fleet. Eventually, the navy placed several hundred warships on blockade duty. But in 1861 nine out of ten vessels got through it to or from Confederate ports.

Gradually, however, the noose tightened, and by the last year of war only half of the ships got through. And these were small, fast, light-draft steam vessels with limited cargo space that were specially designed for blockade running. The exploits of the successful blockade runners helped keep the Confederacy going and earned fame and fortune for their crews. But the Confederacy could never break the blockade, either by diplomacy or by naval power. At sea even more than on land, the North's industrial capacity proved a distinct advantage. While the Confederacy was able to construct several ironclad rams for the purpose of breaking the blockade, these vessels were underpowered, with engines cannibalized from steamboats or from such captured warships as the

GENERAL GEORGE MCCLELLAN, UNITED STATES

USS *Merrimack*. The South simply lacked the capability to build large marine engines, the most complicated technological products of their day.

Deciding early that to maintain an efficient blockade, the navy must have bases along the southern coast, the Union naval strategy board created task forces to seize such bases. In late August 1861, a flotilla shelled Confederate forts on Cape Hatteras into submission and army troops occupied Hatteras Inlet. Two weeks later the navy seized Ship Island off the coast of Mississippi without opposition and used it as a base for the fleet blockading New Orleans and Galveston.

The best natural harbor on the southern Atlantic coast was Port Royal Sound midway between Charleston and Savannah. A task force of fourteen Union warships, accompanied by support vessels and transports carrying twelve thousand soldiers and marines, survived a punishing storm off Cape Hatteras and arrived at Port Royal Sound in early November. Steaming between the two forts guarding the entrance to the sound, the Union warships pounded them mercilessly with accurate gunnery while driving off the small Confederate gunboats which had been nicknamed the mosquito fleet. The forts surrendered; Confederate troops evacuated the coastal islands between Savannah and Charleston; and the Yankees moved in, establishing a large naval base and a small foothold along the South Carolina coast. Subsequent expeditions expanded this foothold to the mouth of the

The young men who enlisted in 1861 soon learned that war was not as eventful as they had expected. Reality was the dull routine of camp life, constant drill in the manual of arms, poor rations, disease, and waiting. There were, of course, various kinds of entertainment including such games of chance as poker, or field games, one which would eventually become the national sport—baseball. For most of the men the war represented the first great adventure away from home, and, as one soldier described it, the experience was "sheer boredom interspersed with periods of sheer terror."

Savannah River and to Florida coastal cities. In February and March 1862, a Union expeditionary force under General Ambrose Burnside supported by naval gunboats gained control of the Albemarle and Pamlico sounds and several port cities along the North Carolina coast.

These events demonstrated the South's vulnerability to Union naval power. In retaliation, the Confederacy tried to destroy Northern merchant shipping with privateers and commerce raiders. Through a loophole in the British neutrality law in 1862, two fast commerce raiders built in Liverpool came into Confederate possession. The two ships, the *Florida* and the *Alabama*, roamed the seas for the next two years, capturing and sinking American merchant ships and whalers. This embittered Anglo-American relations for a long time after the war. The *Alabama* was the most feared raider. Commanded by Raphael Semmes, the foremost Confederate sea dog, she sank sixty-two merchant vessels plus a Union warship before another warship, the USS *Kearsarge* (whose Captain John A. Winslow had once been Semmes's messmate in the old navy) sank the *Alabama* off Cherbourg, France, on June 19, 1864. Nevertheless, the *Alabama* and other commerce raiders and privateers destroyed or captured two hundred and fifty-seven American merchant vessels and drove at least seven hundred others to foreign registry. The American merchant marine never recovered. But while spectacular, this Confederate achievement made only a tiny dent in the Union war effort, especially when compared with the fifteen hundred blockade runners captured or destroyed by the Union navy as well as the thousands of others that did not try to run the blockade. The Confederate navy was never able to challenge Union seapower where it counted: along the coasts and rivers of the South.

The Confederate gunboat *Virginia* was unstoppable. In a single day's action, the captured, refitted, and renamed U.S. ship *Merrimack* had sunk or disabled three Union warships with little damage to herself. On March 9, as the Southern ironclad returned to finish off a ship aground, she was confronted by the Union's own ironclad *Monitor*. For four and a half hours, the ironclads dueled in a slow, lumbering ballet, bouncing iron shot off each other's iron plate. The *Virginia* finally withdrew, leaving the *Monitor* and her blockading fleet to hold Hampton Roads. It was the dawning of a new age in maritime warfare. Neither craft would survive the war, their contribution to the future limited to that one day.

It was not for lack of trying. Although plagued by shortages of every-thing, the Confederate Navy Department demonstrated great energy and innovative skill. Southern engineers developed "torpedoes" (mines) that sank or damaged forty-three Union warships in Southern bays and rivers. They also built small "torpedo boats" to sneak up on Union ships at night and plant a mine next to the hull. One of these, the CSS *H.L. Hunley,* submerged a few feet below the surface and became the world's first combat submarine. In trials, it sank to the bottom three times, drown-ing its crew of six each time (including its inventor, after whom it was named) before venturing out to the blockade fleet off Charleston in 1864. It sank a Union ship but went to the bottom itself for the fourth and last time.

Another Confederate innovation also looked to the future: ironclad warships. The idea of iron armor for ships was not new; the British and French navies had prototype ironclads in 1861. But the Confederacy built the first one to see action. It was the CSS *Virginia,* commonly called the *Merrimack,* even by Southerners, because it had been rebuilt from the steam frigate USS *Merrimack.* This had been burned to the waterline by the Union navy at Norfolk when the Confederates seized the naval base there in April 1861. Finally ready for its trial by combat on March 8, 1862, the *Virginia* steamed out to attack the blockade squadron at Hampton Roads. She sank one frigate with her iron ram and another with the firepower of her eleven guns. Other Union ships ran aground trying to escape, to be finished off the next day (or so the Confederates expected). Union shot and shells had bounced off the *Virginia's* armor plate. It was the worst day for the U.S. Navy until December 7, 1941.

Panic seized Washington and the whole northeastern seaboard. But almost in Hollywood fashion, the Union's own ironclad sailed into Hamp-ton Roads in the nick of time to save the rest of the fleet. She was the USS *Monitor,* completed just days earlier at the Brooklyn navy yard in New York. Much smaller than the *Virginia,* with two eleven-inch guns in a revolving turret (a new invention) set on a deck almost flush with the waterline, the *Monitor* looked like a "tin can on a shingle." But the ship was formidable. She presented a small target and, because of the turret, generated considerable firepower in a given direction. She was also faster and more maneuverable than the *Virginia.*

When the *Virginia* ventured forth on the morning of March 9 to finish off the rest of the blockade squadron, her crew was surprised to see such a strange-looking craft in her way. Thus began history's first battle between ironclads. It was a draw, with neither ship able to inflict crippling damage on the other, but the *Virginia* limped home to Norfolk never again to menace the Union fleet. Two months later, when Norfolk fell to Union forces, the *Virginia's* crew blew her up because her draft was too deep to escape up the James River. Although the Confederacy built other iron-clad rams, some never saw action and none achieved the success initially won by the *Virginia.* By the war's end, the Union navy had built or started building fifty-eight ships of the *Monitor* class (some of them double-tur-reted), launching a new age in naval history that ended the classic "heart of oak" era of warships.

During the early months of 1862, Union naval superiority proved to be a decisive factor in the western theater as well as along the Atlantic

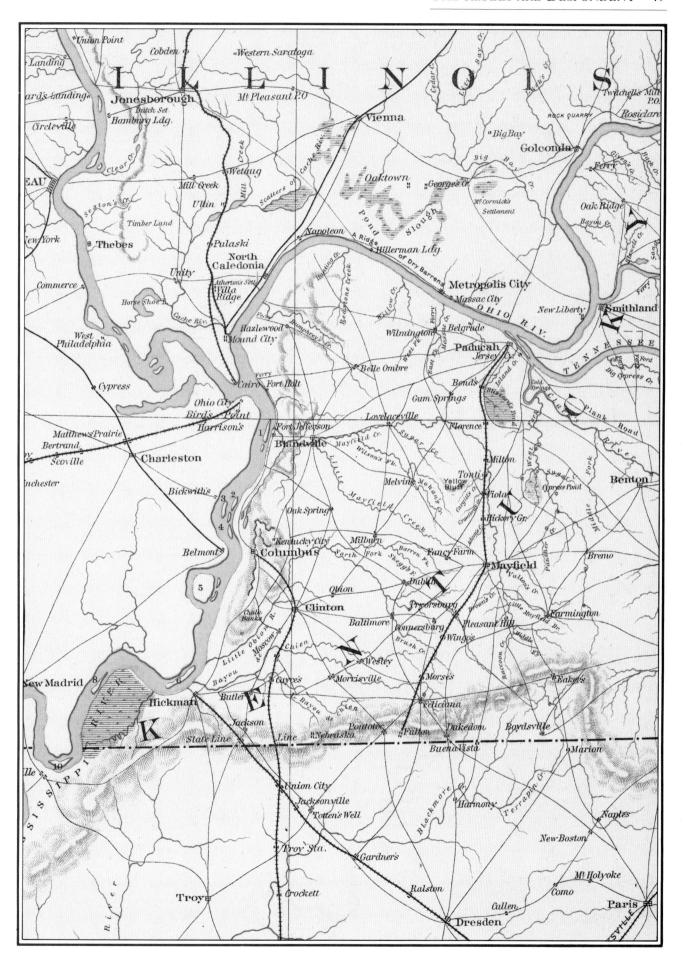

coast. A glance at a map of western Kentucky and Tennessee will reveal the strategic importance of the nexus of four navigable rivers in this region. The Tennessee and Cumberland rivers flow northward from the state of Tennessee through Kentucky and empty into the Ohio River within a few miles of each other. Forty miles to the west the Ohio flows into the Mississippi at Cairo, Illinois, the southernmost place in the free states. The Mississippi, Tennessee, and Cumberland rivers are like three arrows pointing into the heart of the South.

One of the first to grasp the importance of this fact was Ulysses S. Grant, commander of Union troops at Cairo. Grant seemed an unlikely prospect to achieve much in this war. After resigning from the army in 1854 under a cloud that left him with a reputation (largely undeserved) as a heavy drinker, Grant had tried his hand at several civilian occupations with indifferent success. Rejoining the army when war broke out in 1861, he demonstrated a quiet efficiency and determined will that won him promotion from colonel to brigadier general by August 1861. When Confederate units entered Kentucky in September 1861, Grant moved quickly to occupy the strategic mouths of the Tennessee and Cumberland rivers. Unlike McClellan, who had known nothing but success in his career and was afraid to jeopardize that record, Grant's experience of failure made him willing to take risks; he felt he had little to lose. He demonstrated his courage dramatically in the early months of 1862.

Confederate strategists also recognized the importance of this river network. They built forts on the Tennessee and Cumberland rivers where they were only twelve miles apart just south of Kentucky. They also fortified the heights overlooking the Mississippi at the railhead town of Columbus, Kentucky. To penetrate the Confederate heartland, Union forces would have to capture these forts. Grant was eager to try. To help him, the Union War Department converted several steamboats into "tin-clad" gunboats—so-called because they were lightly armored to protect engine and paddle wheels. But the North's main reliance for river warfare was on a whole new class of ironclad gunboats. Carrying thirteen guns, they were flat-bottomed and wide-beamed to draw only six feet of water, with the hull and paddle wheels protected by a sloping casemate sheathed in iron armor up to two and a half inches thick.

When the first three of these odd-looking but redoubtable craft were ready in February, 1862, Grant struck. His initial objective was Fort Henry on the Tennessee River. The gunboats knocked out the fort on February 6 without need of help from Grant's fifteen thousand troops. Fort Donelson on the Cumberland proved a tougher nut to crack. Its guns repulsed a gunboat attack on February 14, demonstrating that these fearsome monsters could be hurt after all by well-aimed artillery. After a miserable night of snow and sleet, the seventeen-thousand-man Confederate army at Fort Donelson tried a breakout attack against Grant's beseiging force, which had been augmented to twenty-seven thousand men. As shivering Northern soldiers were cooking breakfast on that lowering February morning, ten thousand screaming rebels stormed out of the woods to attack on the right. In the hard fighting that followed, a dismounted cavalry battalion commanded by Lieutenant-Colonel Nathan

Bedford Forrest, a Tennessee planter and slave trader with no previous military training who proved to be one of the war's military geniuses, particularly distinguished itself. The Confederate attack punched a hole in Union lines, but a strange lethargy overcame the Southern commanders. They failed to exploit the hole in time to get their men out of the closing trap. Grant calmly organized a counterattack that penned the defenders back up in their lines.

Cut off from support by Grant's superior force on land and by gunboats on the river, the Confederate commander asked for surrender terms on February 16. Grant's reply made him famous: "No terms except an immediate and unconditional surrender can be accepted. I propose to move immediately upon your works." More than two thousand Confederates managed to escape, seven hundred of them under Forrest, whose cavalry crossed an icy creek in the predawn gloom with many infantrymen riding double on the horses. But the other thirteen thousand surviving Confederates surrendered, giving Grant the most striking victory in the war thus far.

Its strategic consequences were far-reaching. Union gunboats ranged all the way up the Tennessee River to northern Alabama, which was occupied by a Union army division, and up the Cumberland River to Nashville, which on February 23 became the first Southern state capital to surrender to Union forces. With their center pierced and Grant's army in their rear, Confederate forces holding a line two hundred miles long through southern Kentucky were compelled to abandon that state and most of Tennessee.

But their commander, Albert Sidney Johnston, was not ready to give up. He concentrated his remaining forces at the rail junction of Corinth in Mississippi just south of the Tennessee border and called in reinforcements from as far away as New Orleans and Pensacola, Florida. With forty thousand men, Johnston planned a counteroffensive against Grant's thirty-five thousand who had established a base twenty miles north of Corinth at Pittsburg Landing on the Tennessee River. Johnston hoped to strike before Grant could be reinforced by troops under Union General Don Carlos Buell. At dawn on April 6 the rebels swarmed out of the woods and hit Yankee lines near a country church named Shiloh. They caught Grant in an embarrassing surprise and drove the unprepared bluecoats toward the river in the bloodiest fighting of the war up to that time. Most soldiers on both sides "saw the elephant" (the Civil War expression for experiencing combat) for the first time in those woods and small clearings between Shiloh Church and Pittsburg Landing (the battle was known by both names for a time, but the Confederate name Shiloh became generally accepted). After fifteen thousand casualties to both sides (more than three times the total at Manassas), Grant's exhausted troops plus the advance units of Buell's arriving reinforcements brought the rebel onslaught to a halt at dusk. One of the Confederate casualties was Johnston, who bled to death when a bullet cut an artery in his leg during the afternoon—the highest-ranking general on either side to be killed in the war. Pierre G.T. Beauregard, who had been transferred earlier from Virginia, took Johnston's place in the midst of the battle.

When the war began Nathan Bedford Forrest, born to an impoverished Tennessee family, had risen to become a wealthy businessman. Raising his own battalion of mounted infantry, the colonel found himself trapped at Fort Donelson, Tennessee. Refusing to surrender with the remainder of the garrison, on February 16, 1862 Forrest and his troops escaped during a blinding winter storm, and forded an ice-swollen river to safety. Forrest would soon receive a promotion to brigadier general for his daring, and continue to achieve notoriety at Shiloh and elsewhere.

Some of Grant's subordinates advised retreat during the dismal, stormy night of April 6–7. Grant would have none of it. "Retreat? No," he said. "I propose to attack at daylight and whip them." Reinforced by three divisions of Buell's army, that is just what he did, driving the Confederates in retreat back to Corinth after nine thousand more casualties to both sides. Once again Forrest's cavalry played a significant role, especially in protecting the retreat against pursuit by the victorious but exhausted and tentative Yankees. Commander of the pursuing brigade was William Tecumseh Sherman, who had fought well as a division commander at Shiloh. But on April 8, at Fallen Timbers, four miles south of Shiloh, Forrest got the best of Sherman by personally leading a wild cavalry charge that broke up the pursuit. Nevertheless, Grant had won a significant victory at Shiloh, even though his reputation suffered a temporary decline because of the grievous Union casualties there (thirteen thousand) and the belief that he had been caught napping the first day.

Union triumphs in the western theater continued during that springtime of Northern hope in 1862. In northwest Arkansas an outnumbered Union force avenged Wilson's Creek by defeating and scattering a Confederate army at Pea Ridge on March 7–8, not only protecting Union control of Missouri but also making significant inroads into another Confederate state, Arkansas. An army-navy task force commanded by General John Pope surrounded and captured seven thousand Confederates at fortified Island No. 10 on the Mississippi River. The Union gunboat fleet continued to fight its way downriver to Memphis, which it captured on June 6 after a spectacular naval battle in which seven of the eight Confederate gunboats were sunk or captured. Pope's army joined Grant's and Buell's for a land campaign against Corinth under the overall command of Henry W. Halleck, highest-ranking Union general in the west. Beauregard evacuated Corinth at the end of May, yielding a strategic rail junction but saving his army.

Perhaps the most dramatic Northern victory in the spring of 1862 was the capture of New Orleans, the Confederacy's largest city and most important port. This, too, was entirely a naval achievement, which started Flag Officer David G. Farragut's and Captain David D. Porter's rise to become the first and second full admirals in the United States Navy. Their campaign against New Orleans was a well-designed operation intended not only to capture that city, but also to open up the soft underbelly of the South and split the western third of the Confederacy from the remainder by gaining control of the whole Mississippi Valley. That underbelly was soft because the South had stripped its Gulf coast of most troops and gunboats to meet the Union advances in Tennessee.

Two strong forts on the Mississippi below New Orleans, an uncompleted ironclad, and a handful of troops were not enough to stop the Yankee sailors commanded by Tennessee-born Farragut. After a weeklong shelling of the forts, Farragut decided on the daring maneuver of running seventeen of his ships past the fort upriver in the predawn darkness of April 24. Despite shot and shell from the forts, and Confederate fire rafts that almost set his flagship afire, Farragut got past the forts with the loss of four ships. He steamed on to New Orleans and compelled surrender of the city with nine-inch naval guns trained on its streets. Fifteen thousand Union troops occupied the city, secured surrender of

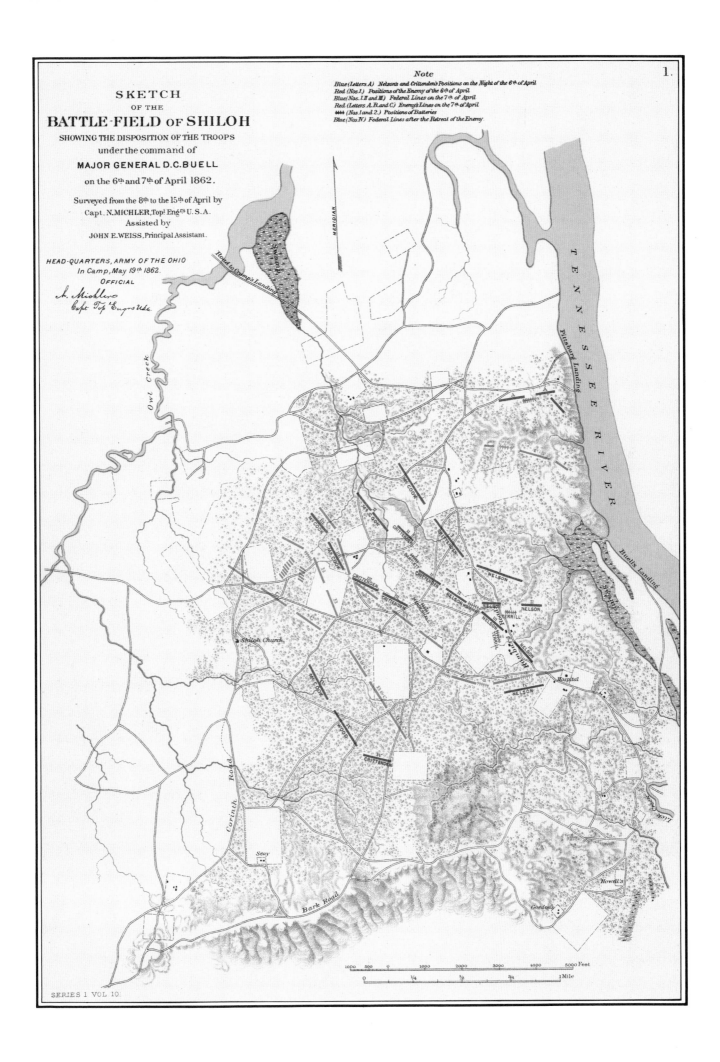

1.

SKETCH
OF THE
BATTLE-FIELD OF SHILOH
SHOWING THE DISPOSITION OF THE TROOPS
under the command of
MAJOR GENERAL D.C. BUELL
on the 6th and 7th of April 1862.

Surveyed from the 8th to the 15th of April by
Capt. N. MICHLER, Topl Engrs U.S.A.
Assisted by
JOHN E. WEISS, Principal Assistant.

HEAD-QUARTERS, ARMY OF THE OHIO
In Camp, May 19th 1862.
OFFICIAL
N. Michler
Capt. Topl Engrs USA

Note
Blue (Letters A) Nelson's and Crittenden's Positions on the Night of the 6th of April.
Red (Nos. I) Positions of the Enemy of the 6th of April.
Blue (Nos. I, II and III) Federal Lines on the 7th of April.
Red (Letters A, B and C) Enemy's Lines on the 7th of April.
(Nos. 1 and 2.) Positions of Batteries.
Blue (Nos. IV) Federal Lines after the Retreat of the Enemy.

TENNESSEE RIVER

Owl Creek

MERIDIAN

Road to Crump's Landing

Pittsburg Landing

Buell's Landing

Shiloh Church

Corinth Road

Bark Road

Seay

Howell's

Gordon's

Hospital

NELSON

CRITTENDEN

COOK

1000 500 0   1000   2000   3000   4000   5000 Feet

0   1/4   1/2   3/4   1 Mile

On April 8, 1862, Colonel Nathan Bedford Forrest was in a fix. Guarding the rear of the retreating Confederate column after Shiloh, he was hounded by a Union party led by General Sherman. Despite a Union advantage in numbers, Forrest chose to charge the advancing foe. Heard shouting "Charge! Charge!" above the din, Forrest led his three hundred and fifty men, including Captain John Hunt Morgan and his Kentuckians, and stopped the Union column. During the ensuing melee, the badly wounded colonel cut his way out, and escaped amidst a hail of bullets as Sherman watched helplessly.

ADMIRAL DAVID GLASGOW FARRAGUT, U.S. NAVY

the forts, and formed the vanguard of a Northern military presence that controlled New Orleans and its rich hinterland for the rest of the war.

Farragut's fleet continued upriver all the way to the Confederate bastion at Vicksburg, where they met the gunboat flotilla that had conquered Memphis and turned it into a Union base. Vicksburg resisted the firepower of these fleets on this occasion. But elsewhere in the west, the string of Union victories from February to June 1862 was uninterrupted. Combined with triumphs along the Atlantic coast and the advance of McClellan's splendidly equipped Army of the Potomac to within five miles of Richmond, these victories had knocked the Confederacy down for the count of nine. "Every blow tells fearfully against the rebellion," boasted the North's leading newspaper, the *New York Tribune,* on May 23, 1862. "The rebels themselves are panic-stricken, or despondent. It now requires no very far-reaching prophet to predict the end of this struggle."

But the *Tribune* proved to be a poor prophet. In Virginia, two rebels who were not despondent stood ready to turn the war around—"Stonewall" Jackson and Robert E. Lee.

III

A
WORSE
PLACE
THAN HELL

GENERAL THOMAS "STONEWALL" JACKSON, CONFEDERATE STATES

LEE AND JACKSON had spent a frustrating winter while Union forces were conquering fifty thousand square miles of the South. Lee had gone to western Virginia in August 1861 to take up his first field command. His task was to drive out Union troops that had occupied the region and were in the process of turning it into West Virginia. But quarreling subordinates, skillful opposition, terrible weather, and the sickness of one-third of his raw troops stymied his plans. He returned to Richmond at the end of October having achieved nothing except a damaged reputation. Jefferson Davis sent him to Savannah to shore up the Confederacy's coastal defenses; Lee arrived the day after the Union navy breached those defenses at Port Royal Sound. The Confederates did manage to prevent further penetration, but when Lee returned to Richmond in March 1862 as President Davis's military adviser, he learned that the main Confederate army in Virginia, under Joseph E. Johnston, had retreated from the Manassas line to a new position south of the Rappahannock to guard against a flank attack up that river by McClellan's army.

The Confederacy seemed everywhere on the retreat in March 1862. In the Shenandoah Valley, Stonewall Jackson's small army of forty-five hundred men pulled back from Winchester in the face of a larger advancing Union force. Jackson had come to Winchester from Manassas in November 1861 to command the Confederate defense of the northern valley. A devout Presbyterian, eccentric in his personal habits, secretive with his associates and subordinates, a stern disciplinarian toward his soldiers whom he expected to share his own indomitable willpower and indifference to creature comforts, Jackson was one of the war's most interesting characters. Many of his soldiers considered him crazy; behind his

Despite his reputation as a stern disciplinarian and devout Christian, Stonewall Jackson was a shy, tender man, wholly devoted to his wife. When duty kept the general at his headquarters at Winchester, Mary Ann often brought him supper in a basket. She would then leave him to work until late into the night. It was the first winter of the war, and in early spring they parted. By the time they saw each other again, thirteen months later, their only child, Julia, had been born.

back they called him "Old Tom Fool," a nickname he had acquired with the cadets at Virginia Military Institute where he had taught for a decade before the Civil War. In January 1862 Jackson had driven his men forward over mountainous terrain in a snowstorm on an expedition to Romney in western Virginia. Protests from a subordinate had caused Jackson to submit his resignation, which the War Department wisely refused to accept.

For if Jackson was crazy, he was also incredibly shrewd. On March 23 he suddenly attacked a larger Union force just south of Winchester. In this battle of Kernstown, Jackson suffered a severe repulse; it was the only battle he ever lost. But the Lincoln administration, reasoning that Jackson would not have attacked unless he had more men in the valley than he actually did have, kept a large Union force there instead of sending some of these troops to reinforce McClellan's developing campaign against Richmond. This decision gave Robert E. Lee ideas. Functioning as a sort of chief of staff for Davis in Richmond, Lee ordered Jackson to carry out diversionary operations in the valley to keep Union troops tied down there and prevent them from reinforcing McClellan. To enable Jackson to do so, the government sent him reinforcements that brought his strength up to seventeen thousand men. One of the reinforcing brigades was commanded by Richard Taylor, a Mexican War hero and the son of President Zachary Taylor. (Taylor made a brilliant record in the Civil War, starting with his part in Jackson's valley campaign of May-June 1862, which became one of the most notable operations of the war.)

In the early spring of 1862, Union forces drove into Virginia determined to capture territory. In the Shenandoah Valley, forces under Stonewall Jackson were successfully parrying Union thrusts below Winchester. But reinforcements were desperately needed. Sent from Richmond, General Richard Ewell's division marched west through the Blue Ridge at Swift Run Gap in a blinding snowstorm. For General Richard Taylor (holding the map) and his sturdy soldiers from Louisiana, it was a harsh introduction to the hazards of early spring marches in Virginia.

Jackson's valley campaign demonstrated the military virtues of deception and fast marching, as well as superior knowledge of the terrain—a constant Confederate advantage, since most of the war took place in their territory. Jackson himself and many of his soldiers were from the Shenandoah Valley. They knew every stream, every hidden hollow and back road. On more than one occasion, Jackson used this knowledge to carry out a feint in one direction and an attack in another, keeping his enemies off balance so that, while the North at one time or another had a total of forty thousand men in the valley, Jackson with seventeen thousand outnumbered his opponents in four of the five battles fought from May 8 to June 9.

During this campaign Jackson marched his men so hard and fast that they became known as Jackson's Foot Cavalry; some of them marched three hundred fifty miles in those thirty-two days. From McDowell, Virginia, north one hundred fifty miles to the Potomac and then the same distance south again to Port Republic, the marching and skirmishing and pitched battles raged as the trees leafed out and the wheat began to ripen in the beautiful Shenandoah Valley. The most decisive battle occurred on May 25 at Winchester, when Jackson's tired men attacked a smaller Union force after a night march and sent them whirling north to the Potomac.

This campaign made Jackson famous. It broke the string of Confederate defeats and boosted Southern morale. Most important, it accomplished its purpose of diverting Union troops to the valley from their main operations against Richmond. Even without these troops, however, McClellan had a significant numerical superiority in these operations from the beginning of April until late June.

The geography of Virginia explains McClellan's strategy in this "peninsula campaign." While the river system in the western theater aided Union invasion, the half-dozen small rivers in Virginia flowing west to east lay athwart the Union line of advance between Washington and Richmond, providing Confederates with natural lines of defense against an overland invasion. Therefore McClellan persuaded a reluctant Lincoln (who insisted on enough troops being left behind to protect Washington) to approve his plan to transport the Army of the Potomac by water down the Chesapeake Bay to the tip of the Virginia peninsula formed by the tidal portions of the York and James rivers. This would shorten the route to Richmond, provide the Union army with a secure seaborne supply line free from harassment by rebel cavalry and guerrillas, and reduce the number of river crossings the advancing Union forces would have to make.

It was a good plan—in theory. And the logistical achievement of transporting one hundred and ten thousand men with their equipment, supplies, and horses and mules to the jumping-off point near Yorktown was impressive. But then McClellan's faults began to undermine the campaign. A small Confederate blocking force at Yorktown held him for the month of April as he cautiously dragged up siege guns to blast a way through defenses that his large army should have punched through in days. When he finally got his big guns in position, the Confederates stealthily abandoned their lines on the night of May 3 before the guns could open fire. A bloody rear-guard battle at Williamsburg on May 5 slowed Union pursuit of the Confederate retreat up the peninsula toward

THADDEUS LOWE

Richmond. Johnston's sixty thousand men established a defensive perimeter only a few miles east and north of Richmond as McClellan closed in on them slowly. And all the while McClellan was bickering with Lincoln and Secretary of War Edwin M. Stanton over the reinforcements they had withheld to cover Washington and to deal with Jackson's rampage through the Shenandoah Valley. Even without the reinforcements, McClellan's army substantially outnumbered Johnston's. But as usual, McClellan had doubled the enemy's strength in his mind, and acted accordingly. Yet his information about enemy numbers and positions should have been better, for he benefited from balloon observation.

Ballooning had become popular in the 1850s, with exhibitions at county fairs and other public events. One of the leading balloonists had the resounding name of Thaddeus Sobieski Constantine Lowe. Early in the war he gained the ear of Lincoln, who was always open to new technologies. On June 17, 1861, Lowe took a captive balloon above Washington; next day he ascended again and sent the first airborne telegraphic dispatch to the ground. Lincoln prodded the reluctant army bureaucracy to create a balloon corps with Lowe as chief of army aeronautics.

Lowe had several balloons with the Army of the Potomac on the peninsula, and he provided McClellan with valuable intelligence. Confederate artillery became the world's first antiaircraft guns, but never succeeded in hitting one of Lowe's balloons. Balloonists again made observations for Union commanders during the Chancellorsville campaign in May 1863. But soon afterward the balloon corps was disbanded and never used again.

As George McClellan's Union army struck toward Richmond, General Nathaniel Banks and his fifteen thousand troops struck southward into the Shenandoah Valley. For Stonewall Jackson and his small force, it was imperative that Banks not be allowed to leave the valley to join McClellan. Beginning in March 1862, Jackson, defeated at Kernstown, rebounded in a series of battles up and down the Shenandoah. On the morning of May 25, he struck at Winchester. Jackson's troops stormed through Union defenses, sending them reeling through town. Riding at the head of his column, Stonewall entered Winchester triumphantly as Banks and his staff scurried out the other end. Townspeople poured into the streets to greet returning sons, brothers, and fathers. It was Jackson's supreme moment of triumph in his Valley campaign.

GENERAL J. E. B. STUART, VIRGINIA

Despite their novelty and the obvious advantages they offered in airborne reconnaissance, balloons suffered from several disadvantages: The heavy, cumbersome machinery that manufactured gas to inflate them limited their mobility and made them useful only when the armies were relatively stationary. The wooded terrain of Virginia limited their value when the trees were in leaf, and they were also useless or dangerous in foggy, stormy, or windy weather. Union officers concluded, as Confederates had long since demonstrated, that good cavalry provided better reconnaissance and intelligence in mobile operations than balloons could. Nevertheless, Confederates never understood why the Yankees abandoned balloons in 1863. "Even if the observers never saw anything," wrote one Confederate general, "they would have been worth all they cost for the annoyance and delays they caused us in trying to keep our movements out of sight."

Despite McClellan's caution, by the end of May his army had advanced to within six miles of Richmond. Under pressure from Davis to do something about this closing ring, on May 31 Johnston attacked McClellan's left wing, separated from the rest of the army by the Chickahominy River. Poor Confederate staff work botched the timing of the attack, and Union reinforcements crossed the flood-swollen river to repulse it. Perhaps the most important consequence of this battle of Seven Pines was the wounding of Johnston. Davis named Robert E. Lee to replace him.

This proved to be a turning point in the campaign. Although many Southerners had little confidence in Lee after the failure of his West Virginia campaign the previous fall, his qualities as a commander immediately manifested themselves when he took over what he renamed the Army of Northern Virginia. He was bold—he had a willingness to take risks, an almost uncanny ability to read the opposing commander's mind, and a charisma that earned him the worship of his men. While McClellan continued to dawdle and to feud with Lincoln about reinforcements, Lee sent his dashing cavalry commander Jeb Stuart on a reconnaissance mission around the whole Union army to discover weak points. Having learned from this that McClellan's right flank north of the Chickahominy was vulnerable, Lee brought Jackson's army from the valley to help with an attack. Jackson and his men, not yet fully rested from their exhausting marches and fighting, proved lethargic in carrying out Lee's orders. Nevertheless, part of the Army of Northern Virginia attacked, on June 26 at Mechanicsville, starting what became known as the Seven Days battles—the heaviest fighting of the war thus far.

In a series of clashes, no single one of which engaged all the forces on each side, Lee kept the initiative, constantly attacking and forcing McClellan to retreat south across the peninsula toward the James River. Only one of the battles—Gaines' Mill on June 27—was a clear Confederate victory, and the last one, at Malvern Hill on July 1, turned into a slaughter of a Confederate frontal assault. Nevertheless, the whole campaign was a significant strategic success for Lee. With eighty-eight thousand men he drove McClellan's one hundred thousand men twenty miles from Richmond and relieved the threat to the capital. This offensive cost the Confederates twenty thousand casualties (compared with sixteen thousand for the Union) and turned Richmond into a vast hospital. But it reversed the momentum of the war.

GENERAL JOHN HUNT MORGAN, ALABAMA

Northern sentiment plunged from the height of euphoria in May to the depths of despair in July. "The feeling of despondency here is very great," wrote a New Yorker, while a Southerner exulted that "Lee has turned the tide, and I shall not be surprised if we have a long career of successes."

The tide turned in the western theater as well during the summer of 1862. Union conquests there proved to be a mixed blessing for the North, for the fifty thousand square miles of conquered enemy territory had to be occupied, defended, and administered, removing thousands of soldiers from Union combat forces. These forces dangled deep in enemy territory at the ends of long rail supply lines vulnerable to enemy guerrilla and cavalry raids. A drought during the summer and fall lowered many rivers below the navigability stage, making Union logistics even more dependent on railroads.

Confederate horsemen were not slow to take advantage of the opportunity. Nathan Bedford Forrest's cavalry wreaked havoc on Union supply depots, railroad bridges, and other vulnerable points. Kentucky cavalry commander John Hunt Morgan, who had recruited a brigade of hell-for-leather troopers among pro-Confederate Kentuckians, proved to be Forrest's equal as a raider behind enemy lines. During July and August, Morgan's merry men crisscrossed Tennessee and Kentucky, covering a thousand miles in twenty-four days and inflicting a great deal of material as well as psychological damage on Union forces and supply lines.

These cavalry operations plus guerrilla raids in the Union rear paved the way for Confederate counteroffensives in the West. The Confederate army that had been driven out of Corinth, Mississippi, in May was split into two parts. After recapturing some territory, Earl Van Dorn's Army of West Tennessee got a bloody nose when it tried and failed to retake Corinth from the Yankees on October 3–4. Meanwhile, at the end of August, Braxton Bragg's Army of Tennessee launched a drive northward from Chattanooga through eastern Tennessee and Kentucky almost to the Ohio River in September before being turned back at the battle of Perryville on October 8. Bragg was forced to retreat all the way back to central Tennessee. But even after these defeats in October, Confederate forces were in better shape in the western theater than they had been four months earlier.

As usual, however, most attention focused on Virginia. The three Union corps near Washington, that were not part of McClellan's Army of the Potomac, Lincoln reorganized into the Army of Virginia under John Pope, who had won plaudits for the campaign that captured Island No. 10 in April. Lincoln also withdrew the Army of the Potomac from the peninsula in August 1862 to reinforce Pope for a drive southward from Washington. Before this could be carried out, Lee seized the opportunity provided by the separation of the two Union armies confronting him, by the ill-will between McClellan and Pope, and by the bickering among various factions in Washington. To attack Pope before a grudging McClellan could reinforce him, Lee shifted most of his army from the peninsula to the Culpeper area in northern Virginia. Jackson's corps had gone first and defeated part of Pope's force in the battle of Cedar Mountain on August 9. Lee then sent Jackson's "foot cavalry" on a deep raid on Pope's rear to destroy the Union supply base at Manassas Junction.

A lively Brigadier General John Hunt Morgan inspected his four thousand mounted riflemen at Alexandria on December 21, 1862. Married just days before, Morgan was about to lead them around the Union forces at Nashville, and northward into what was, for most of them, their native state of Kentucky. Determined to disrupt supply and communication lines to Union forces at Nashville, the bold and dashing Morgan, resplendent in a new gray uniform, was about to make his third, and perhaps his most important foray into Kentucky. The raid would succeed in destroying major railroad bridges, capturing Union supplies and several garrisons, and generally terrifying Union officials in the state. Weeks later, Morgan's weary men returned to find that their raid had not stopped General Rosecrans from venturing out of Nashville to attack General Bragg near Murfreesboro. The joy and exhilaration which Morgan's men felt after their Christmas Raid rapidly diminished in the cold winter snows of Tennessee.

Jackson's men accomplished this mission with style, marching fifty miles in two days. Jackson then went to ground near the old Bull Run battlefield, while Lee hastened to join him with James Longstreet's corps before Pope could attack and overwhelm him. When Pope did find and attack Jackson, on August 29, the Confederate veterans held on grimly along the cuts and fills of an unfinished railroad. Longstreet came up and launched a counterattack on August 30 before most of the sluggish Army of the Potomac could help Pope. Longstreet's attack, joined by Jackson, swept the Yankees back over the same ground of the battle of the previous year, again inflicting a humiliating defeat on the Union army in this second battle of Manassas. The demoralized Union forces retreated into the Washington defenses, where Lincoln reluctantly gave McClellan command of Pope's army as well as the Army of the Potomac and told him to reorganize them into one army.

Despite lack of supplies and the exhaustion of his men, the bold and aggressive Lee decided to keep up the pressure by invading Maryland. On September 4, his weary troops began splashing across the Potomac at a ford forty miles upriver from Washington. Momentous possibilities rode with this move, which took place at the same time as Braxton Bragg's invasion of Kentucky. Maryland might be won for the Confederacy. Another victory by Lee might influence the Northern congressional elections in November, helping Democrats who opposed Lincoln's war policies to gain control of the House and paralyze the Northern war effort—perhaps even force the Lincoln administration to negotiate peace, which would mean Confederate independence. Coming on top of other Confederate successes, the invasion of Maryland might persuade Britain and France to recognize the Confederacy and intervene to end the war—especially since the drastic interruption in cotton imports from the American South had begun to hurt the British economy. (In September 1862, the British and French governments were actually considering an offer of mediation to end the war on terms of Confederate independence. They were awaiting the outcome of Lee's invasion to decide about this initiative.)

Lincoln also awaited the outcome to make a portentous move—an emancipation proclamation. The war had taken on new dimensions since the collapse of hopes for an imminent Union victory in the spring. It had become a total war, requiring mobilization of every resource that might bring victory and destruction of every enemy resource that could be reached. The Confederacy had mobilized its slave population, which constituted a majority of the Southern labor force, to grow food for the armies, work in armaments factories, build fortifications, and perform other vital labor tasks for the Confederate army. For the North to strike against slavery might cripple that crucial Confederate resource. The North could then mobilize part of the freed slave population for the Union by attracting them into the army as laborers, perhaps even as soldiers. This would also add the powerful moral impetus of freedom to the Northern war aims.

Since the beginning of the war, slaves living near Union lines had been voting for freedom with their feet by escaping to Northern army camps. Union General Benjamin Butler, commander at Hampton Roads in Virginia, had admitted several of the fugitive slaves into his lines in

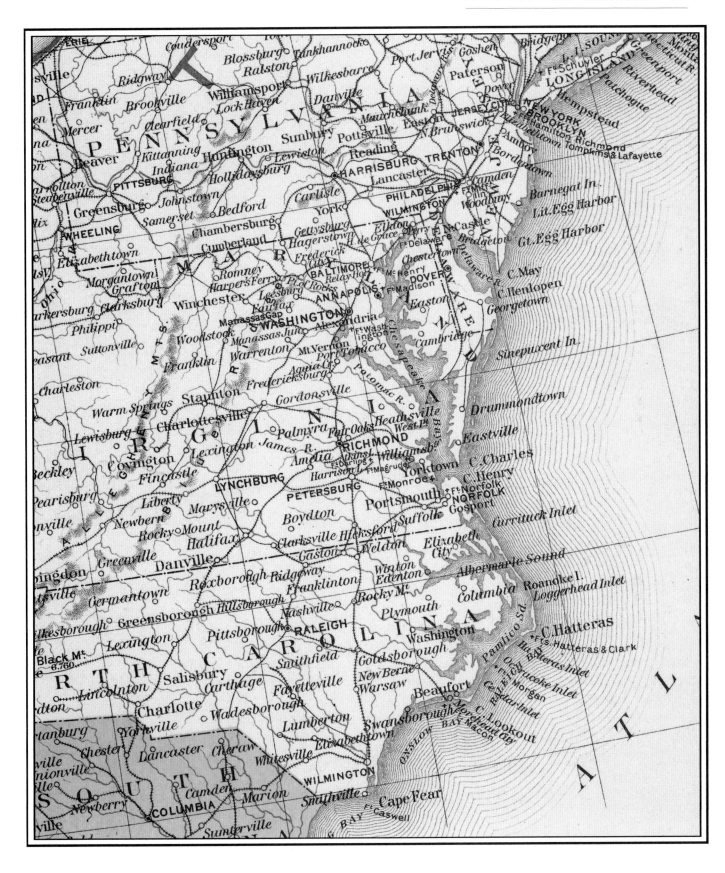

May 1861, pronouncing them "contraband of war"—that is, enemy property subject to seizure under the laws of war. Both the phrase and the concept caught on. Thereafter, slaves who came into Union lines were known as contrabands. In effect they were free, for the Union army put many of them to work for wages.

Pressure grew on Congress and on Lincoln to formalize and expand that freedom by passing legislation or issuing a proclamation to make emancipation a Union war aim. Northern blacks, abolitionists, and a growing number of Republican leaders pointed out that slavery had caused the war and slave labor sustained the Confederate economy. A proclamation of freedom would weaken the Confederacy and strike at the institution that had divided America, shamed its ideals of liberty, and brought the country to the brink of destruction.

As a man deeply committed to opposing slavery, who had many times pronounced slavery a social, political, and moral evil, Lincoln sympathized with these arguments. But as president, he faced constraints on his actions. For one thing, he questioned his or Congress's power to act against an institution protected by the Constitution. For another, he was concerned in 1861 about holding together a fragile coalition in support of the war effort. Lincoln considered it absolutely necessary to keep the three border slave states of Maryland, Kentucky, and Missouri from seceding. Premature action against slavery could drive them into the arms of the Confederacy. It might also drive the Northern Democratic party into opposition to the war. So Lincoln had curbed Union generals who wanted to declare emancipation. He cautioned Republicans in Congress to move carefully. Congress did so, passing confiscation acts (which Lincoln signed) in August 1861 and July 1862 that provided for limited confiscation of enemy property (including slaves) being used to wage war against the United States or belonging to owners who supported the rebellion.

By mid-1862 Lincoln was prepared to go further. The danger of the border states going over to the Confederacy had diminished. The risk of alienating Northern Democrats was outweighed by the opportunity to energize the Republican majority and to mobilize part of the slave population for the Union—and freedom. In July 1862, Lincoln told his cabinet that he now considered emancipation "a military necessity, absolutely essential to the preservation of the Union." The slaves were "undeniably an element of strength to those who had their service, and we must decide whether that element should be with us or against us." Lincoln had overcome his Constitutional reservations; he now believed that his war powers as commander in chief authorized him to seize enemy property—which slaves certainly were. Besides, he said, "the rebels could not at the same time throw off the Constitution and invoke its aid. Decisive and extensive measures must be adopted. We want the army to strike more vigorous blows. The Administration must set an example, and strike at the heart of the rebellion"—slavery.

At an historic meeting on July 22, 1862, the cabinet endorsed the idea of an emancipation proclamation. But Lincoln accepted Secretary of State William H. Seward's advice to delay issuing it until Union arms won a significant victory that could give it credibility and force. The wait proved to be a harrowing one, as Union arms suffered reverses at Cedar Mountain and Bull Run in Virginia and in the initial stages of Bragg's invasion of Kentucky. Thus great issues did indeed ride with the armies as Lee crossed the Potomac and McClellan groped northward to meet him during the second week of September 1862.

For three months everything had gone favorably for the Confederacy. But in mid-September the tide began to turn. The first hint of change came from a bizarre stroke of fortune. Because the Union garrison at Harper's Ferry lay athwart the Confederate supply route from the Shenandoah to Maryland, Lee decided to send a large part of his army to capture it. To do this he split the army into five parts, sending three of them under Jackson's overall command in a pincers' movement against Harper's Ferry and stationing the other two in the valley west of South Mountain in the vicinity of Hagerstown and Boonsboro. On September 9 at Frederick, Maryland, Lee issued several copies of the complicated orders for these movements. One Confederate staff officer whose name is unknown wrapped a copy of the orders around three cigars—and lost them. When units of the Army of the Potomac entered Frederick four days later, a Union corporal found the packet. Up the chain of command it went to McClellan, who understood from these orders that he could pounce on the separated parts of the Army of Northern Virginia before they could unite. McClellan exclaimed: "Here is a paper with which if I cannot whip 'Bobbie Lee,' I will be willing to go home."

As usual, however, McClellan moved sluggishly. On September 14 he drove the outgunned Confederates from two passes in South Mountain. But Lee had learned of the danger and began to concentrate his army at Sharpsburg along high ground between Antietam Creek and the Potomac River. Jackson captured Harper's Ferry on September 15 and rushed most of his men up the river to Sharpsburg. Instead of attacking on the 16th, before most of them could get there, McClellan waited until he had his own forces concentrated to launch an attack the next day. McClellan's caution and tardiness was dictated by his usual overestimate of the numbers facing him. Lee had no more than forty thousand men at Sharpsburg, but McClellan believed he faced at least twice that number with his own force of seventy-five thousand.

McClellan planned to hit the Confederates on both flanks and exploit any resulting weak spot in the center if Lee reinforced his flanks. It was a good tactical plan, but the Union troops did not execute it well. At dawn the Union right under corps commander "Fighting Joe" Hooker swept down the Hagerstown Pike north of Sharpsburg against Jackson's corps on the Confederate left. Vicious fighting raged back and forth through a forty-acre cornfield, along a rocky woodlot known ever after as the West Woods, and in front of a small whitewashed church of the pacifist Dunkard sect. Timely reinforcements from other sectors of the battlefield, plus Jackson's inspiring leadership, enabled the Confederates to prevent a breakthrough in this sector.

General Burnside was commanding the Union left four miles to the south. If he had attacked earlier and more vigorously, or if McClellan had thrown some of his idle reserves against the Confederate center, a breakthrough somewhere could probably have been achieved when Lee shifted troops from those sectors to bolster Jackson on the left. As it was, two Union divisions on the right moved to the center in late morning and

At Antietam, the first Union blow came at 6 A.M., striking toward the left of Lee's dreadfully thin line. In the midst of the battle, General Stonewall Jackson directed the desperate defense, with what an observer described as "his customary imperturbable bravery, riding among his batteries and directing their fire, and communicating his own indomitable spirit to his men." What had made Jackson famous in every battle before was obvious in those desperate, bloody hours as his men were killed and wounded. In a critical moment in the West Woods near the Dunker Church, the unruffled Stonewall directed his final counterattack, saving the Confederate left from complete destruction. Afterwards, as the curious inquired of the condition of his men, Jackson simply replied, "I fear they have done their worst." For General Jackson and the nation, it was the bloodiest single day of the war.

attacked a sunken farm road, known ever after as Bloody Lane, which served as a ready-made trench for the desperate Confederate defenders. After horrendous carnage, in which the famed Irish Brigade of the Army of the Potomac, four New York and Massachusetts regiments composed of Irish-Americans, earned their reputation as one of the hardest-hitting units in the army, the North captured the sunken road. But without support from the reserves withheld by McClellan for fear of a counterattack, they could not exploit this success.

Meanwhile, Burnside had finally gotten his two corps across Antietam Creek and was driving back the Confederate right, threatening to cut off Lee's line of retreat to a ford across the Potomac. At this crisis of the battle, about four o'clock in the afternoon, A. P. Hill's famed division arrived. After a forced march of seventeen miles from Harper's Ferry they pitched into Burnside's flank, bringing the Union advance to a violent halt. Dusk fell on a scene of unparalleled devastation. Twenty-three thousand men were killed, wounded, or missing in twelve hours of fighting, the highest single-day toll in American history. Indeed, casualties in the battle of Antietam (or Sharpsburg, as the Confederates called it) were nearly four times the number of American casualties on D-Day, June 6, 1944.

On September 17, 1862, the solitude of the Maryland countryside was torn apart near the town of Sharpsburg. Repeated Union attacks against Lee's thin left failed, and the Union thrust shifted toward the center. Leading the way was General Thomas Francis Meagher and his "Irish Brigade," composed of immigrants and displaced Irish nationals. Brave and reckless, Meagher's Irishmen surged toward a sunken road on the Piper Farm that was ablaze with Confederate muskets. The green flag of the 69th was riddled. Eight color bearers had already fallen and the Irish green was trailing in the dust. Then Meagher cried out, "Boys, raise the colors and follow me!" Within minutes, the brigade suffered a staggering 60 percent loss, many of the men dying for a country which they had not yet had time enough to know.

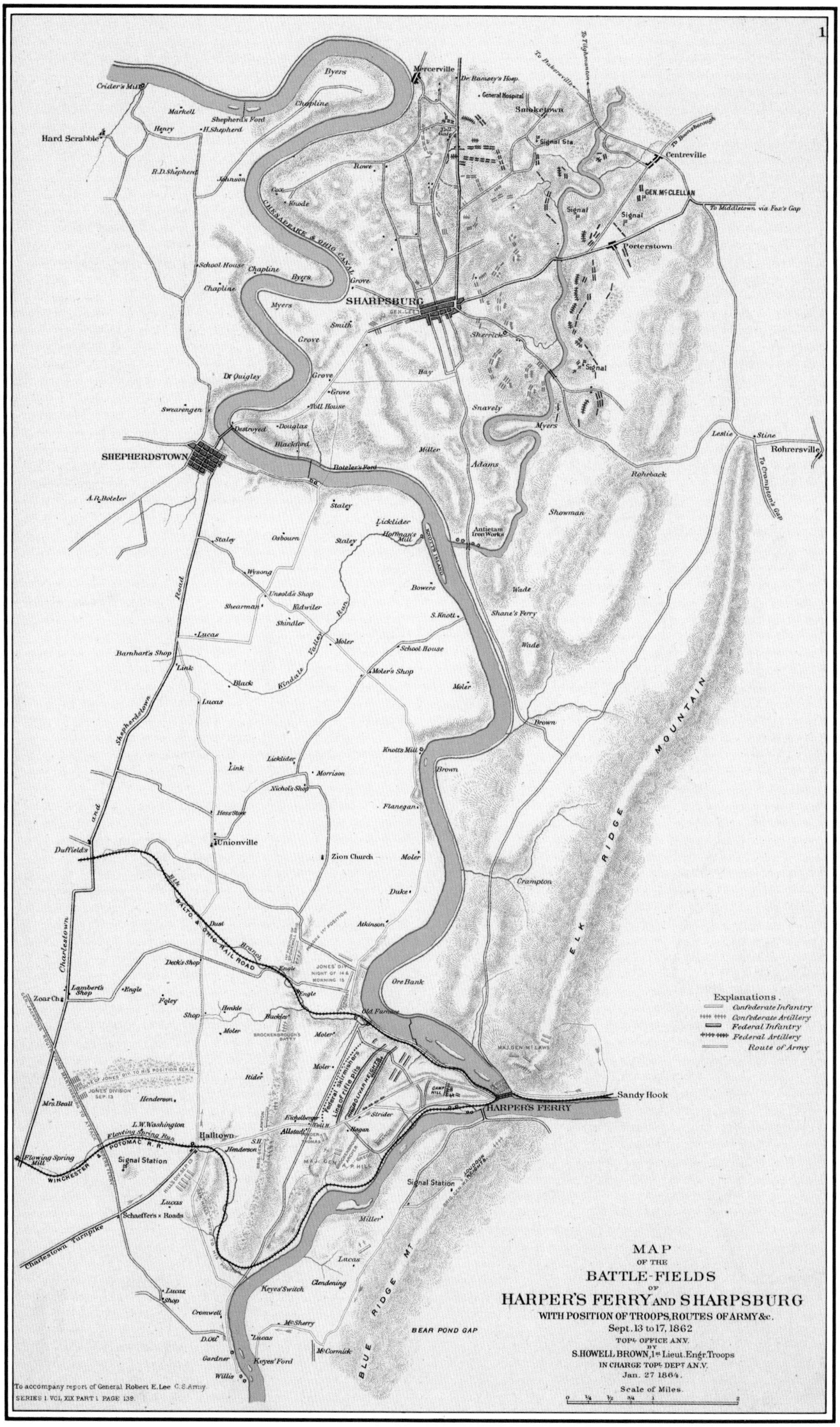

1
MAP
OF THE
BATTLE-FIELDS
OF
HARPER'S FERRY AND SHARPSBURG
WITH POSITION OF TROOPS, ROUTES OF ARMY &c.
Sept. 13 to 17, 1862
TOPL. OFFICE A.N.V.
BY
S. HOWELL BROWN, 1st Lieut. Engr. Troops
IN CHARGE TOPL. DEPT A.N.V.
Jan. 27 1864.
Scale of Miles.
0 1/4 1/2 3/4 1 2
Explanations.
Confederate Infantry
Confederate Artillery
Federal Infantry
Federal Artillery
Route of Army
To accompany report of General Robert E. Lee C.S. Army.
SERIES I. VOL. XIX PART I. PAGE 139.
SHARPSBURG
SHEPHERDSTOWN
HARPER'S FERRY
Mercerville
Smoketown
Centreville
GEN. McCLELLAN
Porterstown
Rohrersville
Sandy Hook
Halltown
Unionville
Hard Scrabble
Crider's Mill
Shepherd's Ford
Boteler's Ford
Antietam Iron Works
Knotts Mill
Zion Church
Flowing Spring Mill
Signal Station
Schaeffers x Roads
Charlestown Turnpike
Shepherdstown and Charlestown Road
BALTO & OHIO RAIL ROAD
WINCHESTER & POTOMAC R.R.
CHESAPEAKE & OHIO CANAL
Kindale Valley Run
ELK RIDGE
ELK MOUNTAIN
BLUE RIDGE MT
BEAR POND GAP
To Middletown via Fox's Gap
To Crampton's Gap

What was achieved by this carnage? Less than might have been. Not only did McClellan fail to commit twenty thousand reserves to exploit potential breakthroughs; he also failed to renew the attack on September 18, even though he received ten thousand reinforcements and Lee received none. And McClellan allowed the battered Army of Northern Virginia, which had lost one-third of its strength in the campaign, to retreat across the Potomac virtually unmolested on the night of September 19–20. But that retreat at least made the battle a Union victory, with far-reaching consequences. Britain and France decided against mediation and diplomatic recognition of the Confederacy. Northern Democrats fell short in their bid to gain control of the House in the congressional elections. Most significant of all, Lincoln seized upon the occasion to issue his emancipation proclamation, on September 22. This was in reality a preliminary proclamation. It warned that in all states or portions of states still in rebellion on January 1, 1863, the President of the United States, acting as commander in chief, would proclaim all slaves "forever free."

Before that date arrived, however, thousands more lost their lives in battle. Although Lee's retreat from Maryland and Bragg's withdrawal from Kentucky a month later looked like a receding Confederate tide, the reversal proved temporary. The Union could never win the war simply by stopping Confederate invasions; Northern armies had to invade the South, defeat its armies, and destroy its ability to resist the authority of the United States.

The three principal Union armies moved sluggishly in November 1862 to attempt just that, two of them under new commanders. Frustrated by McClellan's failure to follow up the victory at Antietam and his slowness to thrust southward, on November 7 Lincoln replaced him with Ambrose Burnside. Burnside started well, getting the army to the Rappahannock River opposite Fredericksburg before Lee could block him. But then things started to go wrong. Pontoon bridges did not keep up with the army, and by the time they arrived at the end of November, Lee with a rested force of seventy-five thousand men had occupied the heights above Fredericksburg. Burnside decided to cross the river and attack on December 13—a disastrous decision, as things turned out. Repeated assaults by courageous Union infantrymen met a hail of lead that produced twelve thousand seven hundred Union casualties, more than twice the Confederate total, and achieved no success whatever. Laments and outcries in the North against this useless sacrifice of life reached a crescendo. A distraught Lincoln told a friend: "If there is a worse place than Hell, I am in it."

News from the West did little to lighten the gloom in Washington. Grant had launched a two-pronged campaign against the Confederate stronghold at Vicksburg. With forty thousand men he penetrated fifty miles into Mississippi by land, while another thirty-two thousand commanded by Sherman moved down the river with the gunboat fleet for an amphibious assault on the heights north of Vicksburg. To counter Grant, Confederates carried out cavalry raids along the railroads and supply depots in his rear, forcing him to retreat toward Memphis at the end of December. From this experience Grant learned an important lesson: Next time he would not depend on vulnerable supply lines to feed his army; he would live off the country while moving through it. Meanwhile

Lying directly between Washington and Richmond, Fredericksburg had been miraculously spared the ravages of war. Yet in November 1862, an ominous foreboding fell over the city as the Union Army of the Potomac appeared across the river. The arrival of Generals Lee and Longstreet on November 20 gave the citizens some hope, which was soon dashed when Lee recommended that for their own safety they leave the city. Two days later, during a blinding snowstorm, the city was evacuated, leaving Fredericksburg to the mercy of the armies. On the morning of December 11, the first Union shells crashed into the houses and shops of the colonial city. Fredericksburg would never be the same.

The signing of the historic Emancipation Proclamation.

Sherman had assaulted the dug-in Confederate defenders at Chickasaw Bluffs on December 29—with no more success than Burnside had had at Fredericksburg.

The only gleam of cheer to the North—and a thin one at that—came from Tennessee as the new year of 1863 opened. General Don Carlos Buell had pursued retreating Confederates feebly after the equivocal Union victory at Perryville, Kentucky, on October 8. A disgusted Lincoln removed Buell from command and replaced him with William S. Rosecrans, who renamed his force the Army of the Cumberland. The day after Christmas 1862 he moved out from Nashville to attack Braxton Bragg's Army of Tennessee thirty miles down the railroad at Murfreesboro. The ensuing three-day battle (called Stones River by the Union and Murfreesboro by the Confederacy) resembled Shiloh in two respects: Confederate success on the first day (December 31) but defeat on the last; and a devastating toll that left both armies crippled for months—twelve thousand nine hundred Union and eleven thousand seven hundred Confederate casualties, one-third of each army. It was the Confederates who retreated, however, to a new base forty miles father south, enabling Yankees to proclaim a victory. Lincoln expressed his gratitude to Rosecrans: "I can never forget, whilst I remember anything, that you gave us a hard-earned victory which, had there been a defeat instead, the nation could scarcely have lived over."

Lincoln learned the news of Stones River shortly after the traditional New Year's Day White House reception at which he had shaken so many hands that his own hand trembled from the strain. Nevertheless, he went to his study after the reception to sign the historic Emancipation Proclamation in the presence of a few friends. As he took up the pen, he later remembered, "I could not for a moment control my arm," which seemed "almost paralyzed." Lincoln paused, "and a superstitious feeling came over me." But he suddenly realized that "I had been shaking hands with several hundred people, and hence a very simple explanation of the trembling and shaking of my arm." Lincoln did not want future generations to read a quavery signature on the proclamation, and say "he hesitated," for "I never, in my life, felt more certain that I was doing right than I do in signing this paper. If my name ever goes into history it will be for this act, and my whole soul is in it." He then took the pen and wrote firmly, without a quaver, "Abraham Lincoln."

With that act, a new day dawned in America. The institution that had mocked American ideals of liberty, divided the nation, and plunged it into internecine war still flourished, to be sure. As a war measure, the proclamation exempted states under Union control. And it did not immediately reach those under Confederate control. But Union armies were now officially armies of liberation. The North now fought for freedom as well as union. If the North won the war, slavery would die. As 1863 opened, however, that remained a big If.

GENERAL ULYSSES S. GRANT, UNITED STATES

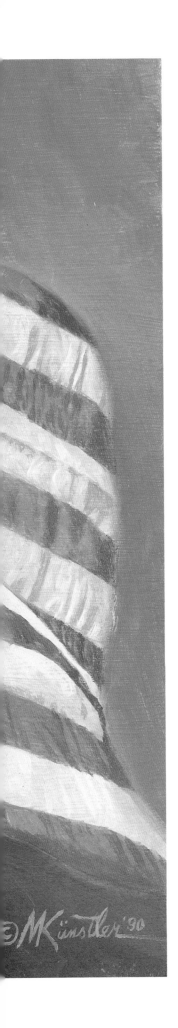

IV

UNVEXED
TO
THE SEA

THE YEAR 1863 WOULD PROVE TO BE a crucial turning point toward ultimate Union victory. But during the first half of the year, things got worse.

In Virginia, General Burnside tried to redeem the disaster at Fredericksburg by launching a movement to cross the Rappahannock River above Lee's defensive line to come in on the Confederate flank and rear. Begun during an exceptional warm and dry spell in January, the movement bogged down in knee-deep mud when the heavens opened and rain turned Virginia's dirt roads into a gluey morass. This ill-fated "Mud March" finished Burnside as commander of the Army of the Potomac. Lincoln replaced him with the aggressive Joseph Hooker, who set about to restore the shattered morale of this hard-luck army.

Grant seemed similarly bogged down in the West during this winter of Northern discontent. Since his first attempt to take Vicksburg was foiled by rebel cavalry raids in his rear, in January 1863 Grant tried a new approach. His strategy was both hindered and aided by geography and topography. Vicksburg was situated on a two hundred-foot bluff on the east bank of the Mississippi that gave Confederate artillery command of the river and rendered a frontal assault suicidal. West of the river a maze of bayous and swamps made military movements difficult if not impossible. East of the river and extending in a two hundred and fifty-mile arc from Vicksburg north to Memphis was a line of hills that enclosed the Delta, a sixty-mile wide network of flood plain and junglelike forest. Only south and east of Vicksburg was there dry land suitable for military operations. Grant's problem was to get there with an army of sufficient size and logistical support to defeat the forces defending Vicksburg and capture this bastion that Confederates labeled "the Gibraltar of the West."

On the map, the simplest way for Union forces to approach Vicksburg was overland from Memphis. But Grant had tried that only to learn the vulnerability of railroad supply in a hostile countryside filled with enemy guerrillas and cavalry. So he decided to use Union naval control of the Mississippi to secure his communications and assist his efforts to land an army on Vicksburg's flank. During February and March, however, Grant's forces floundered through the bayous and jungles in several futile attempts to secure a foothold on high ground. Sickness felled many of Grant's forty-five thousand troops. Criticism of him rose to a crescendo in the North, where the antiwar "Copperhead" faction of the Democratic party gained alarming strength among war-weary Northerners. Worried Republicans pressed Lincoln to remove Grant as he had removed Burnside. But the president had stuck by his most successful general a year earlier when he had been criticized after Shiloh, and he stuck by him now. "I think Grant has hardly a friend left, except myself," Lincoln told his secretary. But "what I want . . . is generals who will fight battles and win victories. Grant has done this, and I propose to stand by him." False rumors about Grant's drinking began to surface again. It was at this time that Lincoln reportedly said that he would like to know Grant's brand of whiskey so he could send some to his other generals.

Grant justified Lincoln's confidence. He ordered the intrepid David D. Porter, who won promotion to admiral for his exploits in this campaign, to run part of his fleet of river gunboats and transports past Vicksburg to protect a crossing by Union troops forty miles below the town. This was a risky move. Even if the fleet got past the guns of Vicksburg with the help of the four-knot current, they would be sitting ducks if they tried to go back up again. Grant's army would have to operate deep in enemy territory without a supply line until they could fight their way back to Vicksburg and reestablish contact with the river north of the Confederate Gibraltar. But like Lee, Grant was a great general because he was willing to take risks. On the moonless night of April 16, eleven of Porter's boats drifted silently down toward Vicksburg. Confederate lookouts spotted them and set bonfires on the shore to give light for their artillerists. The fleets poured on steam and rushed downriver amid a cacophony of big guns and exploding shells. Nearly all of the boats got through. They rendezvoused with the troops on the west bank to ferry them across.

On the last day of April Grant's vanguard was across the river, giving their commander "a degree of relief scarcely equaled since," wrote Grant two decades later. "I was now in the enemy's country, with a vast river and the stronghold of Vicksburg between me and my base of supplies. But I was on dry ground on the same side of the river with the enemy. All the campaigns, labors, hardships, and exposures . . . were for the accomplishment of this one object."

Grant's crossing was virtually unopposed because of two diversions he had ordered to deceive and distract the Confederates. Sherman kept one corps on the Yazoo River north of Vicksburg to feign an attack there that pinned down part of the Southern troops. At the same time, a Union cavalry brigade commanded by General Benjamin Grierson was tearing southward through central Mississippi in a spectacular raid, which demon-

ADMIRAL DAVID D. PORTER, U.S. NAVY

strated that Yankee horsemen had learned from the rebel example.

A former music teacher from Illinois who had disliked horses since one kicked him in the head as a boy, Grierson nevertheless became one of the finest cavalry commanders of the war. Starting from western Tennessee on April 17, Grierson's troopers combined speed, boldness, and cunning as they swept through Mississippi ripping up fifty miles of railroad, capturing two trains at Newton Station seventy miles east of Vicksburg, luring most of the Confederate cavalry and a division of infantry into a futile chase after them, and riding exhausted but happy into Union lines at Baton Rouge after sixteen days and six hundred miles that left the enemy confused and frustrated.

Once across the river, Grant kept the defenders of Vicksburg off balance. Instead of striking due north against Vicksburg, he drove east toward the state capital at Jackson. Grant knew that Joseph Johnston, who had come west as theater commander after recovering from his wounds at Seven Pines, was assembling a force to come to the aid of General John C. Pemberton, commander of the Confederate army at Vicksburg. Grant wanted to eliminate this threat to his rear before turning his attention to Vicksburg itself. On May 1, he cut loose from his supply lines, struck eastward, and told his forty-four thousand troops to live off the country as they marched and fought against two enemy forces whose combined numbers almost equaled their own.

Early on the morning of April 24, 1863, a gray-clad band quietly rode into Newton Station, Mississippi. No one suspected the trouble that these men would be causing the enemy—not the Union, but the Confederacy! They were the Butternut Guerrillas, Union soldiers dressed as Confederates, and the advance party of Colonel Benjamin Grierson's raiding force of seventeen hundred men. At Newton, the guerrillas captured one train, and then pounced upon another, destroying vital supplies meant for Vicksburg. Then they raced into Louisiana. After a ride of six hundred miles in sixteen days, during which the guerrillas wreaked havoc, only twenty-six were killed, wounded, or captured.

Grant's mobility and unexpected maneuvers in what is generally regarded as the most brilliant campaign of the Civil War prevented Pemberton's and Johnston's armies from combining. In two and one-half weeks, Grant's troops marched one hundred eighty miles, fought and won five battles, and penned Pemberton's thirty-two thousand men and three thousand civilians who had remained in town into the Vicksburg defenses between Grant's army on three sides and Porter's gunboats on the fourth. Hoping to capture the works before the debilitating Mississippi summer came on, Grant ordered assaults on May 19 and May 22. But fighting from a network of trenches and artillery redoubts that were stronger than anything yet seen in this war, Confederate troops recovered their morale and repulsed the assaults.

Grant reluctantly settled down for a siege that lasted forty-seven days. He built up his army to seventy thousand men, half of them watching Joseph Johnston who scratched together a force of thirty thousand that lurked several miles in Grant's rear, not daring to attack the stronger Yankees. Pounded and starved into submission, Pemberton surrendered twenty-nine thousand exhausted and emaciated troops on July 4—a coincidence that celebrating Yankees regarded as providential. "This was the most Glorious Fourth I ever spent," wrote an Ohio soldier as Union troops raised the stars and stripes over the courthouse in Vicksburg.

Five days later, the last remaining Confederate stronghold on the Mississippi, the seven thousand-man garrison at Port Hudson, two hundred forty river miles south of Vicksburg, also surrendered. The Mississippi was now a Union highway from Minnesota to Louisiana. "The Father of Waters again goes unvexed to the sea," said Lincoln. The Confederacy had been rent in twain. And Lincoln knew who deserved the credit. "Grant is my man," he said on July 5, "and I am his the rest of the war."

Despite Grant's victories during May and the tightening noose of his siege during June, the reality and portent of events at Vicksburg had not sunk in until the actual surrender. And as always in this war, events in the eastern theater attracted more attention than those in the west. Matters in the east seemed to be going very well for Confederates during the spring of 1863. James Longstreet had taken two divisions to southern Virginia to secure supplies and prevent Yankee incursions in that region. This left only sixty thousand troops at Fredericksburg to defend the Rappahannock line against nearly twice that number. But Lee had strengthened the Confederate defenses against which Burnside had hurled the Army of the Potomac so futilely in December.

Joe Hooker had no intention of repeating that experiment. As warm weather dried the roads in April, he sent two-thirds of his army on a rapid march upriver to cross at lighly defended fords and come at Lee from the flank. This put Lee's sixty thousand in a vice between seventy thousand Union troops advancing eastward to a crossroads hotel named Chancellorsville, ten miles in Lee's rear, and forty thousand across the river in his front. Lee's only apparent choices were to retreat toward Richmond, which would expose his army to possible attacks on both flanks, or to face the army about to meet the larger threat from Chancellorsville, which would risk an attack on his rear from the Union force that could then cross the river at Fredericksburg.

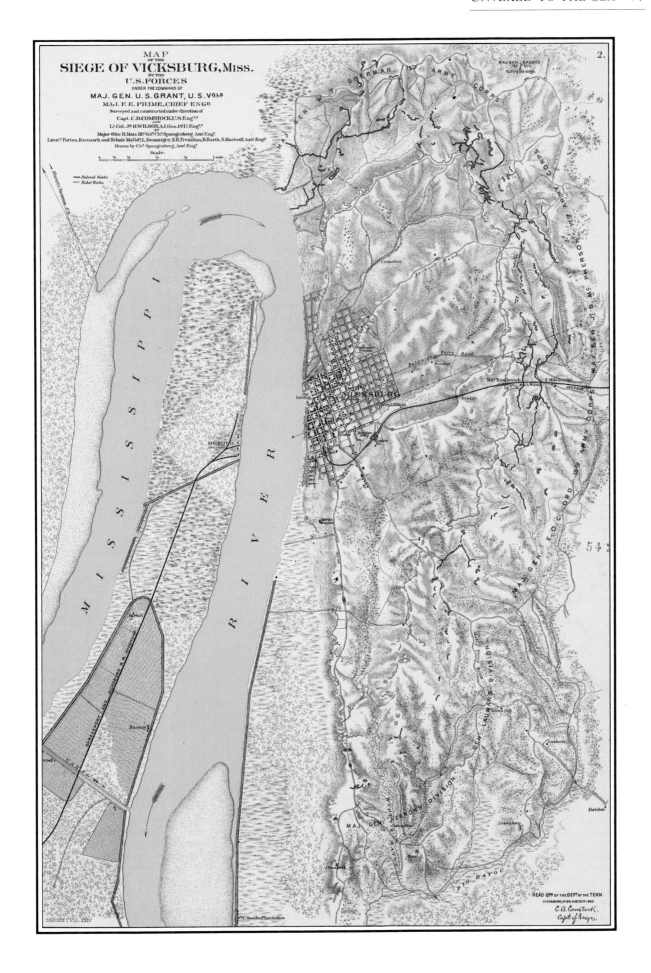

MAP
OF THE
SIEGE OF VICKSBURG, Miss.
BY THE
U.S. FORCES
UNDER THE COMMAND OF
MAJ. GEN. U.S. GRANT, U.S. Vols
MAJ. F.E. PRIME, CHIEF ENGR.
Surveyed and constructed under direction of
Capt. C.B. COMSTOCK, U.S. Engrs.
AND
Lt. Col. Jm. H. WILSON, A.I. Gen. 1st Lt. Engrs.
BY
Major Otto H. Matz, Illm Volm Chm Spangenberg Assm Engrs
Lieutm Patton, Karnasch and Helmle MoVolm, L. Zwanziger, S.R. Tresilian, B. Barth, S. Hartwell, Assm Engrs
Drawn by Chm Spangenberg, Assm Engrs

On July 4, 1863, jubilant Union soldiers marched past the gaunt defenders of Vicksburg and into the city which was the final Confederate stronghold on the Mississippi River. When General Ulysses S. Grant, in his typically informal dress, without swordbelt, rode down to the Old Landing to meet and congratulate Admiral David Porter, commander of the river fleet, aboard his flagship, USS *Benton*, there were more than eight thousand Union troops on hand, cheering, waving flags, and celebrating this great victory. The fall of Vicksburg placed the entire Mississippi River in Union hands.

Typically, Lee did neither. Once again he took a bold risk. He divided his army, leaving General Jubal Early with only ten thousand men to hold the trenches on the heights above Fredericksburg, and took the rest toward Chancellorsville. There the second-growth forest of scrub oaks and pines intertwined with thick undergrowth, known locally as the Wilderness, would tend to neutralize the superior numbers and artillery of the Union troops.

Surprised by Lee's willingness to fight, Hooker yielded the initiative he had so smartly seized. On May 1 he drew back into a defensive posture around Chancellorsville. This was strange behavior for a general previously known as Fighting Joe. But an old army story told of Hooker as a superb poker player "until it came to the point where he should go a thousand better, and then he would funk." In this most deadly game of all, Hooker refused to call Lee's bet.

But Lee still had to show his cards. That night he sat down with Jackson on hardtack boxes in front of a campfire and tried to figure out how to get at the larger Union army entrenched in their front. While they were pondering, Jeb Stuart rode up and reported that his scouts had found the enemy right flank three miles to the west to be "in the air"—unprotected by any natural or man-made defenses, such as a river or fortifications. Lee and Jackson devised a daring plan to

On May 1, 1863, in a small bivouac, illuminated by a campfire, Generals Lee and Jackson were poring over a map, pondering General Joseph Hooker's position. When J. E. B. Stuart arrived with the startling information that the Union flank was open to attack, Jackson immediately proposed that he boldly march his entire corps around to attack the vulnerable point. Lee agreed, fully aware of the risks of dividing his army before the enemy. Lee and Jackson met the following morning for the last time. Within hours, Hooker's forces were routed, and Jackson was mortally wounded, mistakenly, by his own men.

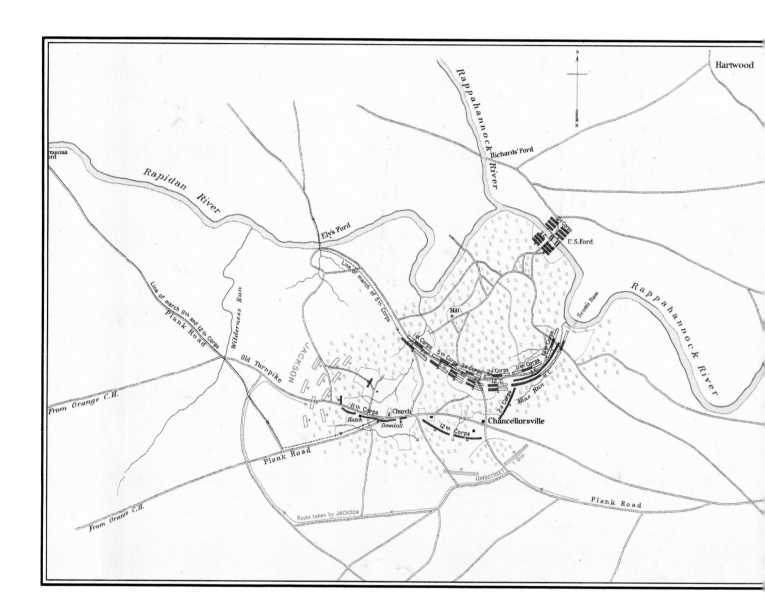

attack that flank. Though the army was already divided, they would divide it again. Jackson would take his corps of twenty-eight thousand men on a circuitous march through the thick woods by back roads known to a local guide and hit the Union flank from the west.

On the morning of May 2, Jackson said good-bye to Lee—for the last time, as it turned out. After an eight-hour march, the attack force deployed in late afternoon. Incredibly, the Yankees had not detected what was going on. Union scouts and skirmishers saw Jackson's troops moving to the south and west. But Hooker allowed wishful thinking to persuade him that the enemy was retreating. Union troops of the 11th Corps—which included many German-American regiments—were resting or cooking supper when Jackson's men burst out of the thickets about 5 P.M. Some of these "Dutchmen" fought valiantly, but they were overborne and swept back in a rout that was finally brought to a halt by Union reinforcements and darkness.

Jackson rode ahead to reconnoiter for a possible attack in the moonlight. As he returned to his own lines he was shot by a jittery squad of Confederate soldiers who mistook him and his staff for Union cavalry. Stuart took command of the corps while Jackson was carried to a field hospital where surgeons amputated his arm. The next day, Lee pressed the attack, winning a bloody victory near Chancellorsville and then turning east to face the Union force coming up from Fredericksburg. After the fourth day of fighting, Hooker acknowledged defeat by retreating across the Rappahannock. Lee had won an incredible victory against odds of nearly two to one. But it had come at the great cost of thirteen thousand Confederate casualties—the greatest of whom was Jackson, who died on May 10 of pneumonia that had set in after he was wounded.

Nevertheless, Chancellorsville further depressed morale in the North, where news of Grant's initial success in the Vicksburg campaign failed to dent despair over events in Virginia. "My God! my God!" exclaimed Lincoln when he learned of the outcome at Chancellorsville. "What will the country say!" And worse seemed to loom on the horizon. Despite the loss of Jackson, the confident Lee decided to invade the North again in a bold bid to conquer a peace on enemy soil.

The invasion got off to an auspicious start—but with consequences that portended trouble. The return of Longstreet's two divisions to the army built up its strength to seventy-five thousand men. Stuart resumed command of his beloved cavalry and held a grand review on June 5 for hundreds of civilians who came out to applaud. Stuart, wrote Lee, "was in all his glory." But four days later, Union horsemen penetrated Stuart's screen and precipitated the largest cavalry battle of the war at Brandy Station. Although the Confederates held firm and finally forced the enemy back across the Rappahannock, Richmond newspapers reproached Stuart and his "puffed-up cavalry" for having been surprised and roughly handled at Brandy Station. This criticism rankled the proud Stuart who considered himself a *beau sabreur*. In his eagerness to redeem himself, he obtained Lee's permission to stage another dramatic raid in the Union rear as the Confederate infantry moved north through the Shenandoah Valley toward Pennsylvania in mid-June. Stuart got carried away by the glory of such an opportunity and rode off on a diverging course from his own army. Separated from Lee's infantry by the Union forces racing

SKETCH
SHOWING THE
POSITIONS OF THE ARMY
ON THE
BATTLE-FIELD
OF
CHANCELLORSVILLE, VA.,
May 1 to 5.
E. F. HOFFMANN,
Lieut. 35th U.S. Inftry.,
late Major, Add. A. de C. on the Staff of Maj. Gen. O.O. HOWARD,
Comdg 11th ARMY CORPS.

Position on May 1st, 4 A.M.
Position on May 3d, 11 A.M.
Position on May 5th, 4 A.M.

Union
Confederate

His was the finest cavalry in the world, and General J. E. B. Stuart wanted to show it. Gathered about the plains south of Brandy Station, the friends and dignitaries invited to the review by the flamboyant Stuart were presented with the spectacle of ten thousand mounted troopers passing in review. They finished with a mock saber charge while shotted cannon fired in salute. Secretary of War Randolph applauded the scene from his private train, as Stuart and his staff bowed and saluted their amazed guests. As they rode to the evening's formal dance, Stuart and his Southern cavalry seemed invincible. Then, four days later, Union cavalry crossed the Rappahannock River and attacked his camps near Brandy Station.

northward, Stuart's weary troops were not able to rejoin the Army of Northern Virginia until July 2, leaving Lee without his cavalry "eyes" during the critical days leading up to the battle of Gettysburg.

At first, however, all went well for the Confederates. Their advance units marched through Maryland and into Pennsylvania all the way to the south bank of the Susquehanna River almost without opposition. This was truly the high tide of the Confederacy. Lee's reputation was at its zenith, exciting awe and admiration abroad and even in the North as well as in the South. He hoped to sustain his army from the rich Pennsylvania countryside, destroy the railroad bridge over the Susquehanna at Harrisburg to cut the North's principal east-west link, and march on Baltimore or Philadelphia or even Washington, perhaps to dictate a victorious peace in the capital.

But Stuart's absence left Lee ignorant of the location of the Army of the Potomac at the end of June. And the Yankees were coming with unwonted speed. A Confederate spy finally got word of this alarming fact to Lee, who ordered his scattered divisions to concentrate at Cashtown, a defensible position in a pass of the South Mountain range. But Gettysburg, a village eight miles east of Cashtown where a dozen roads converged from all points of the compass, turned out to be the actual point of concentration— and the site of the greatest battle ever fought in the Western Hemisphere.

It started the morning of July 1 when a Confederate infantry division ran into two Union cavalry brigades commanded by foresighted General John Buford, who had recognized the strategic importance of the area. Buford's outnumbered troop-

In 1861, Robert E. Lee declined the offer to command the Union army and cast his loyalty with his home state of Virginia. Against great odds, Lee and his Army of Northern Virginia continually outwitted Union strategists. By the summer of 1863, Lee was at the height of his career. Even in the North, he was respected more than some Union generals—a sentiment expressed by one patriotic young Northern woman on the road to Gettysburg: "I wish he were ours!"

ers, fighting dismounted, held off the attacking Confederates until the Union First Corps, commanded by General John Reynolds, arrived in mid morning to stop the Confederate onslaught despite the death of Reynolds with a bullet through his head. Couriers pounded up the roads to summon reinforcements. By afternoon the Confederates managed to concentrate superior numbers north and west of town to win what appeared to be another big victory, driving the North pell-mell through Gettysburg to Cemetery and Culp's hills south of town.

Once again, as at Chancellorsville, it was the hapless 11th Corps that collapsed first, despite the heroics of Captain Hubert Dilger, commander of a six-gun artillery battery. A native of Germany, fondly known as "Leatherbreeches" because of the doeskin pants he liked to wear, Dilger was one of the best artillerists in the Union army, bold and apparently fearless in his close engagements with the enemy. But even Dilger's rapid-firing guns could do little to stem the rout. Lee hoped to keep up the momentum with a late-afternoon attack on the Union rallying point at Cemetery Hill. But Richard Ewell, Jackson's successor as commander of the 2nd Corps, considered the position too strong and did not make the attack.

By the morning of July 2, most of both armies had concentrated near Gettysburg. Viewing the strong Union defensive position anchored by Culp's and Cemetery hills in the north and running south along Cemetery Ridge to two hills known locally as Round Top and Little Round Top, Longstreet wanted to maneuver to the south, toward Washington. This, he said, would compel George Gordon Meade, whom Lincoln had appointed to replace Hooker on the eve of the battle, to attack the Confederates in *their* chosen position.

But Lee would have none of it. His blood was up. He had attacked and won against apparently greater odds at Chancellorsville; he was confident that a re-

It was mid-morning of July 1, 1863, when General John Reynolds rode to the fields west of Gettysburg. Coming upon his old friend John Buford, Reynolds was greeted with the sounds of carbines in the distant fields. "The devil's to pay!" said the imperturbable Buford, and together the two rode to the front. The hard-pressed cavalrymen would have to hold until Reynolds could hurry his men to the field. Left alone, Buford's troopers maneuvered and held back advancing Confederates until Reynolds returned. Sadly, neither Buford nor Reynolds lived long enough to reap any rewards for their decisions on that hot July day. Within the hour, Reynolds was shot dead in the saddle and, several months later, Buford died of pneumonia in a Washington hospital. Their decision to fight at Gettysburg set the stage for the greatest battle of the war, and possibly the most important victory for the Union.

German-born Hubert Dilger came to America just as the war was beginning. With artillery skills honed in Europe, Dilger quickly rose to command Battery "I", 1st Ohio Light Artillery. Nicknamed "Old Iron Pants" because of the leather breeches he wore, Dilger's expertise was quickly put to the test. On July 1, 1863 his gunners were stationed in the fields north of Gettysburg, facing intense artillery fire from several Confederate batteries. Boldly moving several guns forward, the Ohioans flanked and forced back the Southern cannon, Dilger himself, personally sighting the guns in. As the Union infantry broke, Dilger held his men back, covering the withdrawal from the field. In the debacle of the first day's battle, Captain Hubert Dilger's actions were a shining example of bravery and dedication.

GENERAL JAMES LONGSTREET, SOUTH CAROLINA

newal of the attack here at Gettysburg would complete the rout of the enemy begun the previous day and perhaps open the road to Washington. Lee ordered a reluctant Longstreet to assault the Union left. This precipitated fierce fighting at places that became forever famous: the Peach Orchard; the Wheat Field; Devil's Den; Little Round Top. A Mississippi brigade commanded by the fiery politician William Barksdale, his white hair trailing as he led a charge that ended in his death, almost broke through the Union lines on Cemetery Ridge. But they held here and elsewhere on this second day at Gettysburg that saw a turn in the tide of the battle and perhaps of the war.

Despite heavy Confederate casualties and stiffening Union resistance under Meade's skillful tactical leadership, Lee was still confident of victory. Stuart's cavalry had finally rejoined the army along with George Pickett's infantry division, which had not fought the first two days. Believing that Meade had weakened his center to strengthen both flanks, Lee hoped to pierce that center with a three-division assault spearheaded by Pickett's fresh troops. Longstreet again tried to dissuade Lee, telling him that "there never was a body of fifteen thousand men who could make that attack successfully." But Lee disagreed. His men had done it before; why not here? He ordered Longstreet to direct the attack. After a two-hour artillery barrage that did little to soften up the Union center, the Confederate assault—known ever after as Pickett's charge—stepped off at three o'clock on the hot afternoon of July 3. (More than a thousand miles away, at Vicksburg, white flags were at that moment sprouting on Confederate defenses as a prelude to surrender.)

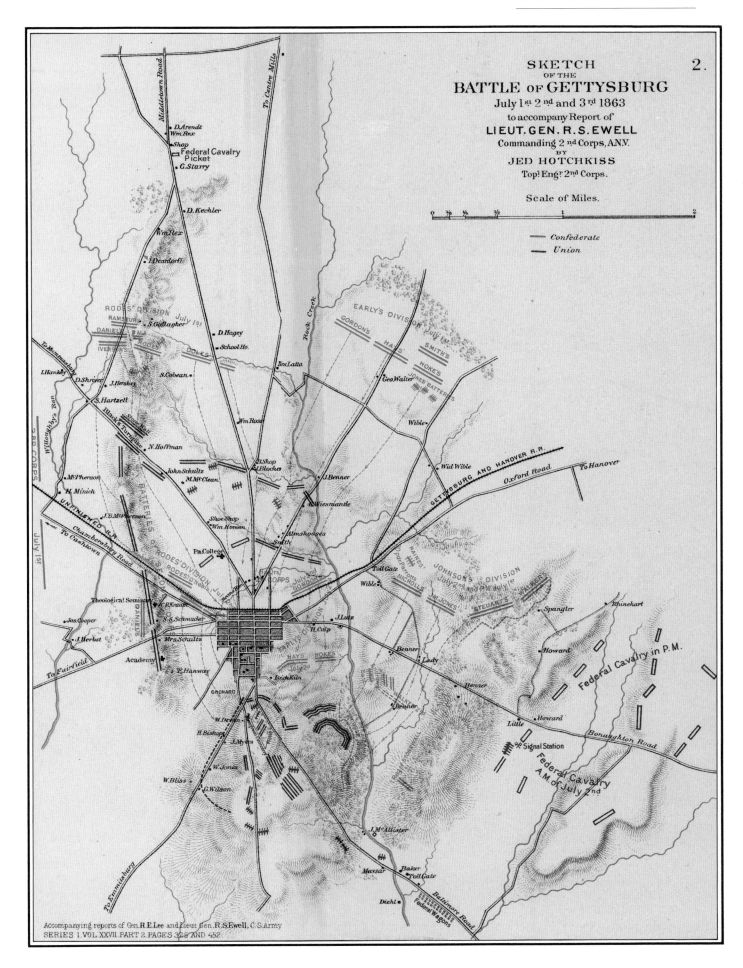

SKETCH
OF THE
BATTLE OF GETTYSBURG
July 1st 2nd and 3rd 1863
to accompany Report of
LIEUT. GEN. R. S. EWELL
Commanding 2nd Corps, A.N.V.
BY
JED HOTCHKISS
Topl Engr 2nd Corps.

Scale of Miles.

2.

_____ Confederate
_____ Union

Accompanying reports of Gen. R.E. Lee and Lieut. Gen. R.S.Ewell, C.S. Army
SERIES I. VOL. XXVII. PART 2. PAGES 325 AND 452.

William Barksdale, senator-turned-general, led his Mississippi brigade into the Battle of Gettysburg with an obsession—to break the Union line. Riding at the head of his men, Barksdale charged straight into and through General Daniel Sickles's thin line. Union reinforcements arrived to block the charge, and Barksdale fell amid a hail of gunfire. But the charge of Barksdale's brigade on the afternoon of July 2, 1863, would forever after be known as the "grandest charge ever seen."

The attackers had to cross three-quarters of a mile of open fields under Union artillery fire almost every step of the way and the massed infantry fire of eight or nine thousand rifles for the final four hundred yards. They never made it. Union lines held firm at the famous angle of a stone fence on Cemetery Ridge and killed, wounded, or captured half of the thirteen thousand Confederates who made the charge. As the survivors limped back to their own lines, they met Lee and Longstreet working feverishly to patch together a defense against the expected Union counterattack. Lee told them: "It's all my fault. It is I who have lost this fight, and you must help me out of it the best way you can. All good men must rally."

But Meade did not counterattack. Bruised by twenty-three thousand casualties, more than one-quarter of his force, he was unaware of how much worse Lee had been hurt, losing at least one-third of the seventy-five thousand men he had brought to Gettysburg. New to the command of the Army of the Potomac, Meade did not want to jeopardize the great victory by hurling his troops against Confederate lines as Lee had hurled his against Cemetery Ridge. So Lee slipped away on July 4, and after several skirmishes during the next ten days, his army escaped across the Potomac to Virginia.

Lincoln was angry with Meade for failing to follow up the victory at Gettysburg with another blow that might have destroyed Lee's crippled army. "My dear general," he wrote to Meade. "I do not believe you appreciate the magnitude of the misfortune involved in Lee's escape. He was within your easy grasp, and to have closed upon him would, in connection with our other late successes, have ended the war. As it is, the war will be prolonged indefinitely." But Lincoln recognized that such a rebuke would cause Meade to resign, which would tarnish the historic victory at Gettysburg and discredit the administration, so he never sent the letter.

Pickett's charge started with a long, gray line in "magnificent order," half a mile wide. But soon the neat ranks were shredded by shot and shell, and they shrank into small groups of men, gathered under tattered red banners. The most determined crossed the Emmitsburg Road, and continued on against Union rifles and cannon which blazed from behind a stone wall. More and more fell, until only handfuls were left. Many surrendered; others turned and ran. It was the end for Lee's plans at Gettysburg, as the Southern tide crested on Cemetery Ridge. The 26th North Carolina would have the honorable distinction of getting the farthest that day. But they paid a terrible price.

Despite Southern dedication and valor, Pickett's charge had failed miserably. As the exhausted survivors stumbled back to Seminary Ridge, Lee, accompanied by his aide, Lt. Colonel Charles Marshall, waited to meet them. He spoke to them with compassion and understanding: "All will come right in the end—we'll talk it over afterwards—we want good and true men just now." To others he confided, "You have done all that men could do; the fault is entirely my own."

At the moment of Lee's most devastating defeat, his greatness and humanity prevailed.

GENERAL JOHN BELL HOOD, TEXAS

Despite Lee's escape, the news of Gettysburg, followed within days by reports of the surrender of Vicksburg and Port Hudson, sent morale in the North from rock-bottom to sky-high. Spirits in the South correspondingly plummeted. Josiah Gorgas, chief of the Confederate Ordnance Bureau, who had almost literally turned plowshares into swords to create an arms industry in the South, wrote in his diary at the end of 1863:

> Events have succeeded one another with disastrous rapidity. One brief month ago we were apparently at the point of success. Lee was in Pennsylvania, threatening Harrisburg, and even Philadelphia. Vicksburg seemed to laugh all Grant's efforts to scorn. Port Hudson had beaten off Banks' force. Now the picture is just as sombre as it was bright then. It seems incredible that human power could effect such a change in so brief a space. Yesterday we rode on the pinnacle of success—today absolute ruin seems to be our portion. The Confederacy totters to its destruction.

This prediction proved premature. But events looked dark enough for the South. For among the "other late successes" noted by Lincoln were advances by Union forces in Tennessee that drove Confederate defenders completely out of the state. After the battle of Stones River at the end of 1862, the two armies in central Tennessee—William S. Rosecrans's Union Army of the Cumberland and Braxton Bragg's Confederate Army of Tennessee—had shadowboxed warily with each other for almost six months as they recovered from the trauma of that battle. After repeated prodding by Lincoln, Rosecrans finally renewed the offensive on June 24. Once they started, his sixty thousand men moved with speed and skill. The forty-five thousand Confederates held a strong position in several passes through the Cumberland foothills. Feinting with his cavalry and one infantry corps toward the westernmost passes, Rosecrans sent three corps through and around the others with such force and swiftness that the Confederates were knocked aside or flanked almost before they knew what had hit them. A brigade of Union mounted infantry armed with the new Spencer repeating rifles got on the railroad in Bragg's rear, forcing the Confederates to retreat all the way to Chattanooga on July 4—the same day Lee retreated from Gettysburg and Vicksburg surrendered. This achievement, without a real battle, cost Rosecrans only five hundred and sixty casualties.

After a pause for resupply, Rosecrans advanced again in August, this time in tandem with a smaller Union army in eastern Tennessee commanded by Ambrose Burnside, who had come to this theater after his removal from command in the East. Again the outnumbered Confederates fell back, evacuating Knoxville on September 2 and Chattanooga on September 9. Lincoln's cherished goal of liberating east Tennessee's Unionists had finally been achieved.

But now Bragg reached into his bag of tricks. Sending fake deserters into Union lines with tales of Confederate demoralization and retreat toward Atlanta, Bragg laid a trap for Rosecrans's troops advancing through the mountain passes south of Chattanooga. To help him spring it, the Davis administration sent Longstreet with two of his divisions from Virginia, one of them commanded by John Bell Hood who had lost none of

his pugnacity despite a wound at Gettysburg that left him with a crippled arm.

On September 19 the reinforced Army of Tennessee turned and struck its tormentors in the valley of Chickamauga Creek. Chickamauga is an Indian word meaning "river of death," and so it proved to be for thousands of Yankees and Rebels during the next two days. The heaviest fighting occurred initially on the Confederate right, where Patrick Cleburne's large division, the best in the Army of Tennessee, launched repeated attacks against the Union left, commanded by George Thomas, one of the stoutest defensive fighters in the Union army. Neither Cleburne nor Thomas fit the conventional mold of their sections: Cleburne was an Irishman who had immigrated to Arkansas in 1849 and felt little commitment to slavery; Thomas was a Virginian who had broken with his family to remain loyal to the Union.

Patrick Cleburne emigrated to the United States in 1849 and settled in Arkansas. In 1861, he began his military career as a private. Two years later, he commanded a division in General Braxton Bragg's Army of the Tennessee. Distinguished in command and ability, Cleburne was at the zenith of his career at the time of Chickamauga, where he led his soldiers into a night attack against a strong Union battle line. Deep in the Georgia wood, Cleburne stood with his men as the muzzleblasts of rifle fire lit up the faces of the combatants. No man could do more to throw the enemy off balance than Cleburne, whom admirers soon called the "Stonewall Jackson of the West."

Northern lines held on the 19th, but the attack erupted with even greater fury next morning. A mixup in orders on the Union side created a gap on the right at just the moment, by coincidence, when Hood's division of Longstreet's imports from Virginia attacked in that sector. Though Hood lost his leg in the fighting, the Southerners achieved a breakthrough here that sent one-third of the Union forces, including Rosecrans himself, reeling in retreat. But the indomitable Thomas kept command of the rest, contracted his lines, stemmed the Confederate onslaught, and protected the retreat of the whole army to Chattanooga on the night of September 20–21. For this feat, Thomas earned the sobriquet "The Rock of Chickamauga."

This battle generated a casualty list second only to Gettysburg: eighteen thousand Confederates and sixteen thousand Unionists killed, wounded, and missing. It was a striking Confederate tactical triumph, but it turned out to be barren of strategic results. Dissension ripped through the Southern command structure, with most of Bragg's subordinates blaming him for failing to follow up his victory and recapture Chattanooga while the Yankees were still disorganized.

The Northern high command, by contrast, responded decisively to the crisis. Lincoln put Grant in overall command of the forces at Chattanooga; Grant in turn replaced Rosecrans with Thomas as commander of the Army of the Cumberland. To reinforce Thomas, the War Department sent twenty thousand troops under Joe Hooker from the Army of the Potomac and seventeen thousand under Sherman from the Army of the Tennessee. Grant went personally to Chattanooga to take charge. By November the momentum, which had seemed to swing back to the Confederates after Chickamauga, went over to the Yankees again.

Bragg's army held four-hundred-foot-high Missionary Ridge east of Chattanooga and eleven-hundred-foot-high Lookout Mountain to the south. These positions, bristling with artillery, seemed impregnable. But Grant knew no such word as *can't*. He developed a coordinated strategy for attacks on both flanks of Bragg's line. On November 24 Hooker launched an assault across the lower slopes of Lookout Mountain in the midst of heavy fog that became known as the Battle above the Clouds. Next morning the rising sun burned away the fog to disclose a huge American flag flying at the summit of Lookout in full sight of both armies below.

This set the stage for Sherman's assault on the north end of Missionary Ridge. Unluckily for Sherman's troops, Cleburne held that end of the line and bloodied the Yankees without yielding an inch. Grant finally ordered Thomas to carry out a limited diversionary attack on the Confederate center to relieve the pressure on Sherman. Led by two divisions that had been routed at Chickamauga and were eager to redeem themselves, Thomas's men carried the first line of Confederate trenches at the base of Missionary Ridge. Then spontaneously, without orders, the Yankees began to move up the ridge in the face of apparently worse odds than Pickett's men had faced at Gettysburg. Watching in amazement from his command post, Grant asked, "Thomas, who ordered those men up the ridge?"

Equally bewildered, Thomas replied, "I don't know."

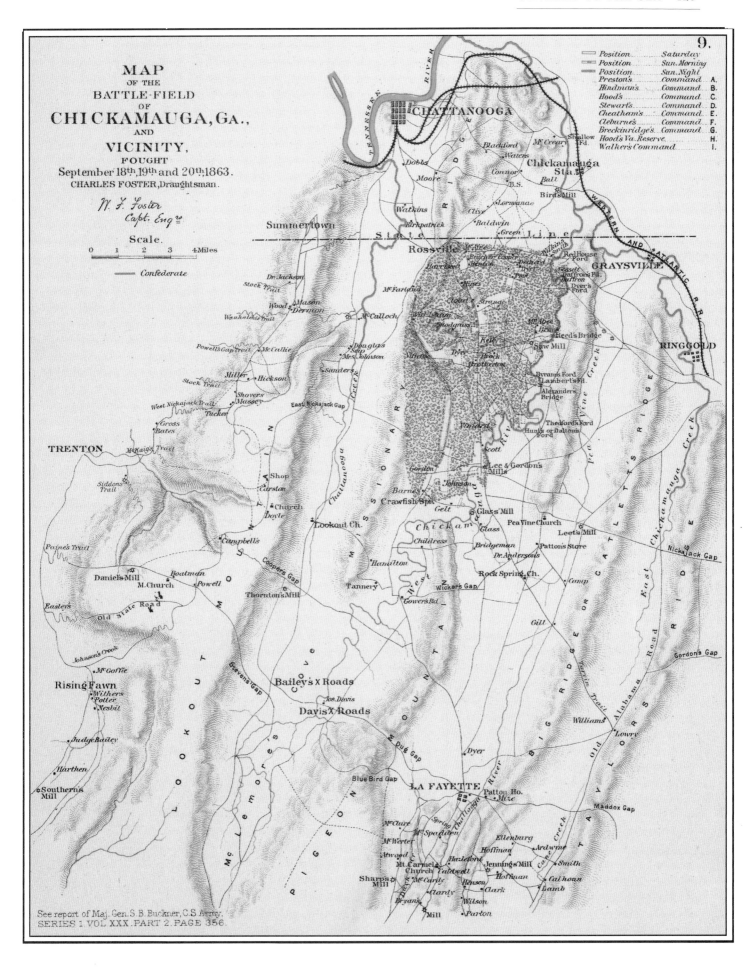

9.

MAP
OF THE
BATTLE-FIELD
OF
CHICKAMAUGA, GA.,
AND
VICINITY,
FOUGHT
September 18th, 19th and 20th, 1863.
CHARLES FOSTER, Draughtsman.

W. F. Foster
Capt. Eng.re

Scale.
0   1   2   3   4 Miles

— — Confederate

	Position	Saturday
	Position	Sun. Morning
	Position	Sun. Night
Preston's	Command	A.
Hindman's	Command	B.
Hood's	Command	C.
Stewart's	Command	D.
Cheatham's	Command	E.
Cleburne's	Command	F.
Breckinridge's	Command	G.
Hood's Va. Reserve	....	H.
Walker's Command	....	I.

See report of Maj. Gen. S. B. Buckner, C. S. Army.
SERIES 1. VOL XXX. PART 2. PAGE 356.

Overlooking Chattanooga, Lookout Mountain was the anchor of Braxton Bragg's left flank. On the morning of November 23, 1863 troops led by Joseph Hooker bridged Lookout Creek and swept the face of the mountain. Among the rocks and tangled growth, Bragg's Confederates fought desperately, while fascinated observers in Chattanooga strained to see through the smoke which covered the fighting. Aptly named, the "Battle Above the Clouds" opened the door to Confederate defenses on Missionary Ridge.

The men had ordered themselves. Sixty regimental flags seemed to be racing each other to the top. The ravines and woods of the slope offered cover that made the assault less foolhardy than it appeared. And Bragg's defensive line at the top was poorly laid out. As the Yankees kept coming, the demoralized defenders panicked, broke, and fled in an utter rout. It was the most decisive tactical victory of the war—and one of the few successful frontal assaults.

This tactical success had important strategic consequences. It completed a cycle of victories begun at Gettysburg and Vicksburg that made 1863, a year in which the Confederacy had at first seemed destined to win the war, a year instead of "calamity . . . defeat . . . utter ruin" in the words of one Confederate official. Mary Boykin Chesnut, the Southern diarist, found "gloom and unspoken despondency hanging like a pall everywhere." Chattanooga was the gate to Atlanta and the deep South. Having cut the Confederacy in two at Vicksburg and Port Hudson, Union forces now stood poised to cut it in three with a thrust through Georgia. Jefferson Davis removed the discredited Bragg from command and reluctantly replaced him with Joseph Johnston, in whom Davis had little confidence. In March 1864 Lincoln summoned Grant to Washington and appointed him general in chief of all Union armies. This signified a fight to the finish.

Events of 1863 also confirmed the abolition of slavery as a Union war aim. The Northern people had not greeted the Emancipation Proclamation with universal acclaim. Quite the contrary; Democrats and border-state Unionists denounced it, and Democrats scored gains in the 1862 congressional elections by campaigning against emancipation. Many Union soldiers resented the idea that they would now be risking their lives for blacks. This issue intensified a morale crisis and a rise of the desertion rate in Union armies during the early months of 1863. Racism in the North remained a powerful obstacle.

But one spinoff of emancipation eventually helped to overcome this obstacle. The Lincoln administration committed itself to the enlistment of freed slaves —and free black men—in the Union army. Like emancipation, this policy encountered initial skepticism and opposition. So the administration proceeded cautiously. Loyal Northerners "have generally become willing that [blacks] should fight," commented the *New York Tribune* on May 1, 1863, "but the great majority have no faith that they will really do so. Many hope they will prove cowards and sneaks—others greatly fear it."

One of the strongest proponents of recruiting black soldiers was the radical Republican governor of Massachusetts, John Andrew. He took the lead in recruiting a model black regiment, the 54th Massachusetts. Desiring the most experienced and committed abolitionists as white officers of this regiment, Andrew named as its colonel Robert Gould Shaw, son of a prominent abolitionist family. Two of the sons of the foremost black abolitionist, Frederick Douglass, joined the regiment—one of them as its sergeant major. When the 54th completed its training and marched through Boston on May 28, 1863, to embark for the South Atlantic theater, Andrew presented the colors to Shaw with the words: "I know not, Mr. Commander, when, in all human history, to any given thousand men in arms there has been committed a work at once so proud, so precious, so full of hope and glory as the work committed to you. I stand or fall, as a man and a magistrate, with the rise or fall in history of the Fifty-Fourth Massachusetts Regiment."

The 54th Massachusetts Infantry was the first volunteer black regiment raised in the North. The ranks were filled with former slaves and freedmen, all sharing the same dream of serving their country. Under the tutelage of its firebrand colonel, Robert Gould Shaw, the 54th became a model of perfection in drill and camp. Their true test came in battle, a suicidal assault on Battery Wagner on the South Carolina coast. Killed on the ramparts of the fort, Shaw was buried in an unmarked grave with the casualties of his regiment.

The 54th justified his confidence. On July 18 it led a Union assault on Fort Wagner, part of the network of Confederate defenses protecting Charleston. Though the attack failed, the 54th fought courageously, suffering 50 percent casualties, including Colonel Shaw killed with a bullet through his heart. "Who asks now in doubt and derision, 'Will the Negro fight?'" commented one Northerner. This battle "made Fort Wagner such a name to the colored race as Bunker Hill had been for ninety years to the white Yankees," observed the *New York Tribune.* "Through the cannon smoke of that dark night," said the *Atlantic Monthly,* "the manhood of the colored race shines before many eyes that would not see."

Many Democratic eyes still refused to see; the party campaigned on an anti-emancipation platform in several crucial off-year state elections in 1863—for governor of Pennsylvania and Ohio and for the legislature of New York. In a public letter supporting Republican candidates, Lincoln set the tone for his party's commitment to freedom and black soldiers. Addressing the foes of these policies, he wrote:

> You say you will not fight to free Negroes. Some of them seem willing to fight for you. Some of the commanders of our armies in the field who have given us our most important successes, believe the emancipation policy, and the use of colored troops, constitute the heaviest blow yet dealt to the rebellion. [When final victory is achieved] there will be some black men who can remember that, with silent tongue, and clenched teeth, and steady eye, and well-poised bayonet, they have helped mankind on to this great consummation; while, I fear, there will be some white ones, unable to forget that, with malignant heart, and deceitful speech, they have strove to hinder it.

Republicans carried the 1863 election by decisive margins. It was a vote for emancipation. If the Emancipation Proclamation had been submitted to a referendum a year earlier, observed a newspaper editor in November 1863, "the voice of a majority would have been against it. And yet not a year has passed before it is approved by an overwhelming majority." This transformation provided a theme for Lincoln's address at the

President Lincoln was invited to deliver "a few appropriate remarks" at the dedication of the new National Cemetery at Gettysburg. It was a cool November day when the president gave the brief speech, completed just the evening before. Replying to featured speaker Edward Everett's lengthy oration, Lincoln believed his brief comments had been a failure. History has proved them the most powerful and persuasive words he ever spoke.

dedication of a national cemetery for Union soldiers at Gettysburg on November 19. That new nation founded four score and seven years earlier had been "conceived in Liberty, and dedicated to the proposition that all men are created equal." Yet the United States had become the world's largest slaveholding country, a mockery of those ideals of liberty. Now, however, Lincoln said, "we are engaged in a great civil war" not only to preserve the nation from destruction but also to ensure that "this nation, under God, shall have a new birth of freedom."

That new birth of freedom received a powerful impetus when the Senate on April 8, 1864, passed the Thirteenth Amendment to the Constitution to abolish slavery. Democrats in the House blocked the required two-thirds majority for the amendment there. The Republicans endorsed it in their platform for the 1864 presidential election. But the ultimate fate of the Thirteenth Amendment depended on the outcome of the war. The year 1864 would see the grinding campaigns and showdown battles that determined this outcome.

The Emancipation Proclamation of 1862 was the beginning of the dream of freedom for thousands of Americans living in bondage. On January 31, 1865, the Thirteenth Amendment was finally passed after a bitter, year-long struggle through Congress. The amendment freed all persons, north and south, from the bonds of slavery. It gave a new purpose to the Union cause, and further reason for the South to fight on.

V

THE
DEEP WATERS
ARE
CLOSING
OVER US

PRESIDENT ABRAHAM LINCOLN

Northern leaders faced the military campaigns of 1864 with confidence. The momentum of victory in the second half of 1863 augured well. A potentially serious problem had been solved: More than half of the three-year volunteers of 1861 had reenlisted. Without these veterans, the Union army might have sputtered to a halt during the summer of 1864. The War Department had appealed to their patriotism and pride—but had also offered monetary and psychological incentives in the form of a four-hundred-dollar bounty and a thirty-day furlough. The chance to visit home again before resuming the fighting in which many of them might be killed was a powerful inducement; one hundred thirty-six thousand Union veterans signed on for another three years.

Confederate veterans had no choice; legislation compelled them to stay in the army until they were carried out on a stretcher or the war ended. The South faced dire prospects during the winter of 1863–1864. Although "I have never actually despaired of the cause," wrote a War Department official in Richmond, "steadfastness is yielding to a sense of hopelessness." But Robert E. Lee did not despair. He recognized that Grant's appointment as general in chief of Union armies meant a relentless offensive against the Confederacy. To counter it, Lee's strategy for 1864 was to hold out long enough and inflict enough casualties on enemy forces to demoralize the Northern people. This would encourage the rise of a peace party to challenge Lincoln's reelection and to negotiate peace with the Confederacy. "If we can break up the enemy's arrangements early and throw him back," explained General Longstreet, "he will not be able to recover his position or his morale until the presidential election is over, and then we shall have a new president to deal with."

Grant was aware of this Southern plan. He hoped to crush Confederate armies and win the war well before November. His strategy was elegant in its simplicity. While smaller Union armies in various peripheral theaters would carry out harassing and diversionary campaigns, the two principal armies would attack Lee in Virginia and Joseph Johnston in Georgia. Grant would go with the Army of the Potomac personally, although Meade remained titular commander of that army. Grant put his most trusted subordinate, William Tecumseh Sherman, in command of Union forces in northern Georgia.

The soldier's life was a melancholy one; songs and stories always evoked thoughts of home. North and south, few young men had been away from home before the war. The Confederate soldier could rarely get time away from the army. In the Northern armies, furloughs were granted for re-enlisting, and gave soldiers a chance to return to their loved ones for a few days. For so many, it was the last time they would ever see home.

GENERAL WILLIAM TECUMSEH SHERMAN, UNITED STATES

Convinced that in previous years the Union armies in various theaters had "acted independently and without concert, like a balky team, no two ever pulling together," Grant ordered simultaneous offensives on all fronts, to prevent Confederates shifting reinforcements from one theater to another. "Lee's army will be your objective point," Grant told Meade. "Wherever Lee goes, there you will go also." At the same time he directed Sherman "to move against Johnston's army, to break it up and to get into the interior of the enemy's country as far as you can, inflicting all the damage you can against their war resources."

The coordinated offensives began in the first week of May. Once again the heaviest fighting and the strongest glare of publicity occurred in Virginia. As the Army of the Potomac crossed the Rapidan into the scrub oak forest known as the Wilderness, where Joe Hooker had come to grief exactly a year earlier, Lee decided to attack the Union flank before the enemy could emerge into more open country south of the Wilderness. This brought on two days (May 5 and 6) of the most confused and ferocious fighting the war had yet seen. Hundreds of wounded men burned to death in fires started in the underbrush by muzzle flashes and exploding shells. The fighting surged back and forth with no clear advantage to either side—although perhaps Lee could claim a victory by bringing the Union offensive to a bloody halt with nearly eighteen thousand casualties —compared to twelve thousand Confederates who had been killed, wounded, or captured.

Many Union soldiers, veterans of the battle of Chancellorsville in these same tangled woods, considered it another defeat. When Grant ordered a move on May 7 that initially took part of the army toward the Rappahannock, they thought it was another retreat across that river. But when they reached a crossroads and turned *south*, the men realized that a new hand was at the helm. "Our spirits rose," one Yankee soldier later wrote. "We marched free. The men began to sing." Grant had promised Lincoln that "whatever happens, there will be no turning back." Now he proved that he meant it. As Grant cantered by the Union troops slogging southward by the light of the burning Wilderness that night, the men cheered wildly even though they knew he was leading them to another killing field.

Grant's objective was the road junction at Spotsylvania Courthouse a few miles to the south. But Lee had divined his intention and rushed troops there only minutes ahead of the advancing Union. On May 8 the clash for this vital crossroads began, escalating into a twelve-day battle that left another eighteen thousand Yankees and twelve thousand Rebels killed, wounded, or captured. This time the Confederates fought from trenches and breastworks they had constructed virtually overnight. Both armies had learned the advantages of entrenchment, which gave the defense an enormous advantage and made frontal assaults almost suicidal. By the time the war was over, Virginia—and Georgia, too—would look as if a race of giant moles had burrowed their way through the countryside.

Grant made several attempts to smash through or around these defenses. His greatest success came at dawn on the foggy morning of May 12, when a whole Union corps broke through the apex of the Confederate trench line, capturing twenty cannons and several thousand men. With his army in danger of being sliced in two, Lee called up his reserve division

The 1864 campaign had ground to a fiery halt in the inferno of the Battle of the Wilderness. For two days, Union and Confederate soldiers fought in an area of dense woods, interspersed with tangled thickets and small farm fields. Fires, kindled in the dry underbrush, added another element of horror to the battle as helpless wounded were burned alive. By the end of the second day, every Union soldier acknowledged the next move: north, once again in defeat. Instead, the tired columns were turned southward, toward Richmond. Through the column rode the new architect of their campaign, General Ulysses S. Grant. Colonel Horace Porter, who rode with Grant, wrote, "Wild cheers echoed through the forest. Men swung their hats... and pressed forward to within touch of their chief, speaking to him with the familiarity of comrades." The veterans knew that this nondescript general was as determined to finish the war as they were. For Grant, it was a victory. For Lee, it was a new and more dangerous adversary.

GENERAL JOHN BROWN GORDON, GEORGIA

commanded by John B. Gordon, a fighting thirty-two-year-old officer who had been promoted up the ranks from captain to brigadier general. Alarmed and excited, Lee proposed to lead Gordon's troops personally in a counterattack. "General Lee," said Gordon, "this is no place for you. Go back, General; we will drive them back." Gordon's men took up the cry, knowing that if Lee was hit or captured their cause was lost. "General Lee to the rear; Lee to the rear!" they shouted. Lee finally consented, and watched while Gordon skillfully directed a slashing counterattack that contained the Union breakthrough.

All day on that terrible May 12, savage combat raged along several hundred yards of Confederate trenches that became famous as the Bloody Angle of Spotsylvania. Individual Union soldiers jumped on the parapet and fired into the trenches as fast as comrades could pass loaded rifles up to them, until they were shot down. Killed and wounded men lay in the trenches so thickly that many were trampled under the muck of mud and blood. The intensity of the firing cut down mature trees as well as men. "I never expect to be fully believed when I tell what I saw of the horrors of Spotsylvania," wrote a Union officer, "because I would be loath to believe it myself were the case reversed."

The Confederates held on grimly at the Bloody Angle and on subsequent days at Spotsylvania. Recognizing that he could not break through there, Grant decided to make another flanking movement to the left. Lee again anticipated him, shifting his army to a new defensive line at the North Anna River halfway between Spotsylvania and Richmond. After probing these lines, Grant again sidled to the left, to Totopotomoy Creek and then to the crossroads tavern at Cold Harbor, near the site of the 1862 Gaines' Mill battle, less than ten miles from Richmond. Believing the Confederates demoralized and exhausted from their repeated retreats, Grant decided to attack on June 3—a costly mistake, as it turned out. Lee's troops were ragged and hungry, but they were far from demoralized. Fighting from trenches that anticipated those of World War I in their strength and complexity, they decimated the Union assault, inflicting seven thousand casualties in half an hour. "I regret this assault more than any other one I have ordered," said Grant afterward.

While all this was going on, Grant had sent his cavalry under General Philip Sheridan on two raids deep into the Confederate rear. Only thirty-three years old, Sheridan's rise had been even more meteoric than John B. Gordon's on the other side. Languishing as a quartermaster captain as late as May 1862, Sheridan got command of a cavalry regiment in the western theater and proved so effective ("he is worth his weight in gold," wrote a superior) that he was promoted to command an infantry division by September. His division fought superbly at Perryville and Stones River; it was caught in the rout at Chickamauga but redeemed itself by leading the miraculous charge at Missionary Ridge.

Grant brought Sheridan east with him to take command of the Army of the Potomac's cavalry, which he turned into one of the crack units of the war. In May, this cavalry carried out a raid to the outskirts of Richmond, cutting the rail lines supplying Lee at Spotsylvania and mortally wounding Jeb Stuart himself in a battle at Yellow Tavern on May 11. While at Cold Harbor, Grant sent Sheridan on another raid, this time toward the rail lines to the west of Richmond. He was intercepted by

Grant's thrust out of the Wilderness was blocked at Spotsylvania Courthouse, where desultory fighting turned the battlefield into a maze of trenches. One section of Lee's line around the village was in the shape of a giant "mule shoe," as the soldiers called it. After an early attempt to break through the mule shoe failed, on May 12 Generals Grant and Meade committed two entire corps to another attack. In rain and dense fog, Union soldiers overran the Confederates in their earthworks, severing Lee's line. Desperate moments followed until a Confederate counterattack drove back the attackers, and the fighting became perhaps the most intense and bloody of the war. With only a log and earthen wall separating them, the combatants shot, stabbed, and clubbed each other for almost eighteen hours. The most furious fighting centered around a slight angle in the earthworks, where the intense rifle fire was thick enough to chip away the trunk of an oak tree. Lee's Southerners held on while engineers built a new line behind them. Darkness finally ended the fighting, and the next morning a Union officer crept up to the "Bloody Angle" to find: "Hundreds of Confederates, dead or dying, lay piled over one another in those pits. The fallen lay three or four feet deep in some places. . . . The trenches were nearly full of muddy water. It was the most horrible sight I had ever witnessed." Few episodes were ever to equal the horrors of Spotsylvania.

Confederate horsemen, now under the command of Wade Hampton, at Trevilian Station, where a two-day battle raged along the railroad and ended in a draw.

In the meantime, Grant had again moved around Lee's flank to the left, this time all the way across the James River to Petersburg twenty miles south of Richmond. Once more Lee's troops raced on the inside track to block the Yankees, for the loss of the rail junction at Petersburg through which most supplies from the south reached Richmond would force the Confederates to abandon their capital. Four days of Union assaults on the desperately defended trenches at Petersburg produced eleven thousand Northern casualties but no breakthrough. Union losses in the previous six weeks had been so high—sixty-four thousand killed, wounded, and missing—that the Army of the Potomac had lost its fighting power. Grant reluctantly settled down for a siege at Petersburg that would last more than nine grueling, murderous months.

In Georgia, Sherman's campaign against Johnston seemed to have achieved more success at less cost than in Virginia, but it, too, had bogged down in an apparent stalemate by August. The strategy and tactics of both commanders in Georgia were different from those in Virginia. Grant and Lee favored attack and all-out battle as a means of destroying the enemy. Sherman and Johnston engaged in a war of maneuver. Grant in Virginia constantly forced Lee southward by flanking moves to his left, but only *after* bloody battles. Sherman forced Johnston back toward Atlanta by constantly flanking him to the Union right, generally *without* big battles.

General Philip Sheridan, short and fiery with a hot Irish temper, came east with the goal of using the Union cavalry as a formidable fighting force—an army unto itself. When, in 1864, he was given command of the Army of the Shenandoah, the cavalry was its heart and soul. More than just soldiers, they were Sheridan's men.

Much of the strategy of this campaign was dictated by the geography and topography of northern Georgia, a region of rugged mountains interlaced by swift rivers and narrow passes through which ran the few roads and the single-track railroad between Chattanooga and Atlanta, on which both the Union and Confederate armies depended for their supplies. Sherman's goal was to strike the railroad in Johnston's rear and force him to fight or retreat. Johnston usually chose to retreat.

Through May and June the two armies executed maneuvers interspersed with skirmishes and small battles that resembled nothing so much as the intricate steps of a minuet. They confronted each other at such previously obscure places as Rocky Face Ridge, Resaca, Cassville, and Allatoona Pass. Sherman sidestepped gracefully to his right, Johnston stepped back to conform, and after nodding to each other they repeated the process. Sherman's fourth major flanking movement brought the armies to equally obscure places only twenty miles from Atlanta where Sherman attacked and the Confederates parried: New Hope Church, Pickett's Mill, Kenesaw Mountain.

By the end of June, Sherman had advanced eighty miles at the cost of seventeen thousand casualties—only one-quarter of Grant's losses in Virginia. Johnston had suffered even fewer casualties, fourteen thousand, compared with Lee's thirty-five thousand. But the Davis administration and Southern public opinion had become alarmed by Johnston's apparent willingness to yield territory without a fight. When Sherman flanked the Confederate defenses again the first week of July, crossing the Chattahoochee River and forcing Johnston back to Peachtree Creek less than five miles from the center of Atlanta, the axe fell. On July 17 Davis removed Johnston from command and replaced him with John Bell Hood, who had stayed with the Army of Tennessee after recovering from the amputation of his leg at Chickamauga.

Hood had learned his trade as an aggressive division commander under Lee. He intended to practice Lee's tactics in Georgia. Three times from July 20 to 28 he attacked Sherman's encircling army: north of Atlanta at Peachtree Creek on July 20, east of the city in the battle of Atlanta on July 22, and to the west at Ezra Church on July 28. Each time the Confederates reeled back in defeat, suffering thirteen thousand casualties to Sherman's six thousand in the three battles. Hood pulled back into Atlanta's defenses and essayed no more attacks. But his cavalry and infantry did manage to keep Sherman's troops off the two railroads into Atlanta from the south. Like Grant at Petersburg, Sherman seemed to settle down for a siege.

By August the Confederate strategy of holding out until the Union presidential election and wearing down the Northern will to continue fighting appeared to be working. Union casualties on all fronts during the past three months totaled a staggering one hundred thousand. "STOP THE WAR!" shouted Democratic headlines. "Who shall revive the withered hopes that bloomed at the opening of Grant's campaign?" asked the leading Democratic newspaper, the *New York World*. "All are tired of this damnable tragedy. If nothing else would impress upon the people the absolute necessity of stopping this war, its utter failure to accomplish any results would be sufficient."

Even Republicans joined the chorus of despair. "Our bleeding, bank-rupt, almost dying country longs for peace," wrote Horace Greeley, editor of the leading Republican newspaper, the *New York Tribune*. The shrewd politico Thurlow Weed observed in August that "the people are wild for peace. Lincoln's reelection is an impossibility." Lincoln thought so, too. "I am going to be beaten," he told a friend, "and unless some great change takes place, *badly* beaten."

In August the Democratic national convention nominated the popular George B. McClellan for president on a peace platform. "After four years of failure to restore the Union by the experiment of war," it declared, we "demand that immediate efforts be made for a cessation of hostilities." Southerners were jubilant. Democratic victory on this platform, said the *Charleston Mercury*, "must lead to peace and our independence" if "for the next two months *we hold our own and prevent military success by our foes.*"

To add insult to injury, Confederate forces carried out harassing raids into Union-controlled territory. In mid-June Lee had detached Jackson's old corps, now commanded by Jubal Early, from the Petersburg front for another campaign through the Shenandoah Valley. Meeting feeble oppo-sition, Early marched northward, crossed the Potomac, and marched to the outskirts of Washington on July 11 and 12 before he was forced to retreat.

In northern Mississippi, Forrest's cavalry had defeated a larger Union force at Brice's Crossroads on June 10 and threatened to cut Sherman's rail supply line through central Tennessee. Although another Union army defeated his troopers and wounded Forrest himself at Tupelo, Missis-sippi, on July 14, the "Wizard of the Saddle" recovered and continued to rampage through central Tennessee and northern Alabama.

In Georgia, Hood ordered his cavalry commander, Major General "Fightin' Joe" Wheeler, who had not yet reached his twenty-eighth birthday, to carry out a raid on Sherman's rail lifeline from Atlanta back to Nashville. Starting north on August 10, Wheeler ripped up many miles of track in northern Georgia and eastern Tennessee, then swerved west al-most to Nashville, where he dismantled some more railroad before head-ing south again.

Though spectacular, Wheeler's month-long raid accomplished less than it should have. Sherman's engineer corps repaired the rail line al-most as quickly as Wheeler's men destroyed it. Skirmishes with Union pursuers and the exhaustion of broken-down men and horses took a fear-ful toll; Wheeler returned with barely two thousand of the forty-five hun-dred men he had when he started. And worst of all, from the Confederate viewpoint, the absence of this cavalry from the Atlanta front worked to Sherman's advantage when he launched the move that would prove to be the war's final and decisive turning point.

At the end of August, Sherman's mobile infantry again swung to the right to attack Hood's rail supply line twenty miles south of Atlanta. At the battle of Jonesboro on August 31 and September 1, they succeeded. Hood had no choice but to abandon Atlanta on the night of September 1 after blowing up and burning everything of military value in the city. The next day Union troops marched into Atlanta, whose symbolic as well as

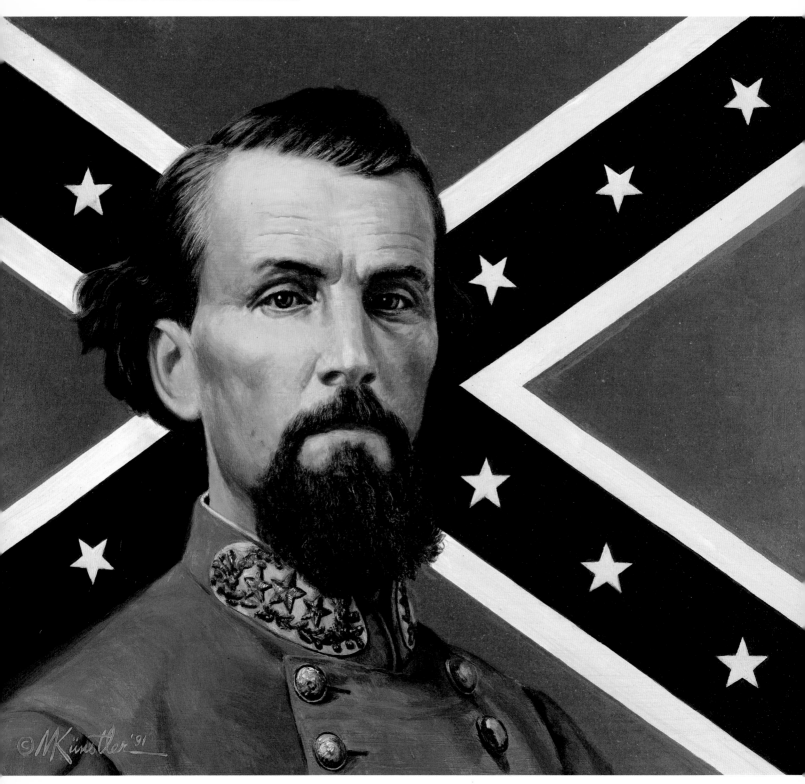

GENERAL NATHAN BEDFORD FORREST, TENNESSEE

substantive value to the Confederacy had become second only to Richmond's. Sherman sent a jaunty telegram to Washington: "Atlanta is ours, and fairly won."

This news had an enormous political impact. "VICTORY!" blazoned Republican headlines. "IS THE WAR A FAILURE? OLD ABE'S REPLY TO THE DEMOCRATIC CONVENTION." A New York Republican wrote jubilantly that the capture of Atlanta, "coming at this political crisis, is the greatest event of the war." The *Richmond Examiner* provided a Confederate perspective on the fall of Atlanta: it "came in the very nick of time" to "save the party of Lincoln from irretrievable ruin. It will obscure the prospect of peace, late so bright. It will also diffuse gloom over the South."

And if Atlanta were not enough to turn around Lincoln's prospects for reelection, events in the Shenandoah Valley completed the job. After Jubal Early's raid through the valley all the way to Washington in July, Grant had put Philip Sheridan in charge of a reinforced Army of the Shenandoah and told him to go after Early "and follow him to the death." Sheridan was the man for the job. He injected the same aggressive spirit into the three Union infantry corps of the Army of the Shenandoah that he had already done for his cavalry. On September 19 he attacked Early a few miles east of Winchester, and after a daylong battle culminating in an old-fashioned cavalry charge that crumpled the Confederate left, the Union sent Early's outnumbered army "whirling through Winchester," as Sheridan put it in a telegram to Washington, "and we are after them tomorrow." He was as good as his word, pressing on after the retreating Confederates and attacking them again on September 22 at Fisher's Hill twenty miles south of Winchester. Once more the Confederate line collapsed; Early's army fled sixty miles southward. This enabled Sheridan to carry out the second part of his assignment in the valley that had twice served as a Confederate route of invasion, that helped feed Lee's army, and that sheltered Rebel guerrillas: to destroy the valley's crops and mills so thoroughly that "crows flying over it for the balance of the season will have to carry their provender with them."

Sheridan did this with a vengeance. In October he wired the War Department that by the time he was through, "the valley, from Winchester up to Staunton, ninety-two miles, will have little in it for man or beast." The Union cavalry did most of the destruction. It also whipped Early's cavalry in several skirmishes and one spirited battle at Tom's Brook on October 9. Returning northward to Cedar Creek, fifteen miles south of Winchester, Sheridan prepared to return part of his army to Grant at Petersburg, and went personally to Washington to consult about future plans. But Early was not willing to lie down and play dead. Reinforced by a division from Lee, he launched a surprise attack across Cedar Creek at dawn on October 19 that caught the Yankees napping in Sheridan's absence. Until noon on that hazy October day the Confederates had everything their own way. But Sheridan, who had spent the night at Winchester on his way back from Washington, arrived personally on the battlefield and took charge. His extraordinary charisma and tactical leadership turned the battle from a Union defeat into another Confederate rout. In late afternoon the whole Union line swept forward in a counterat-

As Lee and Grant faced each
other over the siege lines at
Petersburg, Jubal Early's Confederate army prowled the Shenandoah Valley. Sent to clear the
valley once and for all, General
Philip Sheridan began a ruthless
campaign. His Army of the Shenandoah battered Early at
Winchester, Fisher's Hill, and
Cedar Creek. The Union cavalry, under the direction of such
auspicious commanders as
Wesley Merritt and George
Armstrong Custer, equally shattered Confederate cavalry
screens in hundreds of skirmishes and small encounters.
Time was running out for the
Confederacy, and for the Shenandoah—the bread basket of
Virginia.

tack that shattered Early's divisions and ended any effective Confederate presence in the valley—this time for good.

In retrospect it became clear that the one-two punches of Sherman and Sheridan had knocked out the Confederacy. They certainly ensured the reelection of Lincoln by a landslide on November 8. This was an endorsement of Lincoln's policy of relentless war to the bitter end— unconditional surrender of the Confederacy. Especially notable was the soldier vote in this election. Most states had passed laws allowing absentee voting by soldiers at the front. Despite the lingering affection of some of them for their old commander McClellan, an extraordinary 78 percent of the soldiers voted for Lincoln—compared with 55 percent of the civilian voters. The men who would have to do the fighting had sent a clear message that they meant to finish the job.

Many Southerners got the message. But Jefferson Davis did not. The Confederacy remained "as erect and defiant as ever," Davis announced. "Nothing has changed in the purpose of its government, in the indomitable valor of its troops, or in the unquenchable spirit of its people." It was this last-ditch defiance that Sherman set out to break in his famous march from Atlanta to the sea.

Sherman had long pondered the nature of this war. He had concluded that "we are not only fighting hostile armies, but a hostile people." Defeat of Confederate armies was not enough to win the war; the railroads, factories, and farms that supplied these armies must be destroyed. The will of the civilian population that sustained the armies must be crushed. Sherman expressed more bluntly than anyone else the meaning of total war. He was ahead of his time in his understanding of psychological warfare—and he was in a position to practice it. "We cannot change the hearts of those people of the South," he wrote, "but we can make war so terrible and make them so sick of war that generations would pass away before they would again appeal to it." In Tennessee and Mississippi, Sherman's troops had burned and destroyed everything of military value —and much else besides—that was within their reach. Now Sherman proposed to do the same in Georgia. He urged Grant to let him cut loose

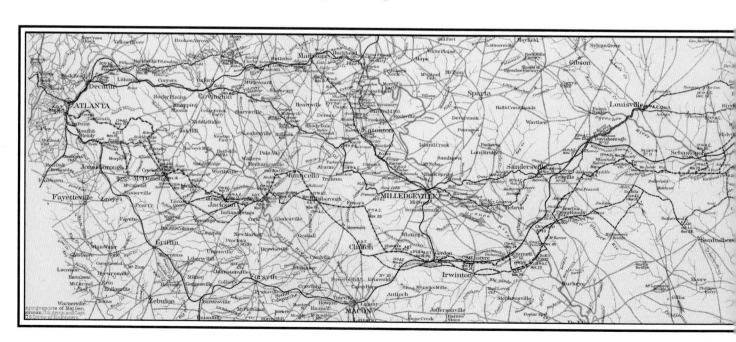

from his base in Atlanta and march his army through the heart of Georgia, living off the land and destroying all the resources not consumed by the army—the same policy on a much larger scale that Sheridan had carried out in the Shenandoah Valley. The psychological impact of such a campaign, said Sherman, would be greater even than its material effect. "If we can march a well-appointed army right through [Jefferson Davis's] territory, it is a demonstration to the world that we have a power which Davis cannot resist. This may not be war, but rather statesmanship."

Grant and Lincoln were reluctant to authorize such a risky move, especially with Hood's army of forty thousand men still intact and hovering in northern Alabama ready to move into Tennessee if Sherman marched away in the opposite direction. But Sherman promised to send George Thomas with forty thousand men to Tennessee where in addition to Union divisions already there, they would be more than a match for Hood. With the remaining sixty thousand troops Sherman could "move through Georgia, smashing things to the sea. . . . I can make the march, and make Georgia howl!"

Lincoln and Grant finally consented. On November 16, Sherman's avengers marched out of Atlanta after burning everything of military value in town. Inevitably, the flames spread and consumed one-third of the city. Sherman and his soldiers cared little; in their opinion the rebels had sown the wind and deserved to reap the whirlwind. Southward they marched toward Savannah, destroying or consuming everything in their path that could possibly be considered of military value in a swath fifty miles wide and two hundred eighty miles long. On December 21 these Yankee troops entered Savannah and Sherman telegraphed Lincoln: "I beg to present you, as a Christmas gift, the city of Savannah, with one hundred fifty heavy guns and plenty of ammunition, and also about twenty-five thousand bales of cotton."

Sherman's march had encountered little opposition because instead of following him, Hood had invaded Tennessee with the hope of recovering that state for the Confederacy. But this campaign turned into a disaster that virtually destroyed Hood's army. As Thomas with the main part of

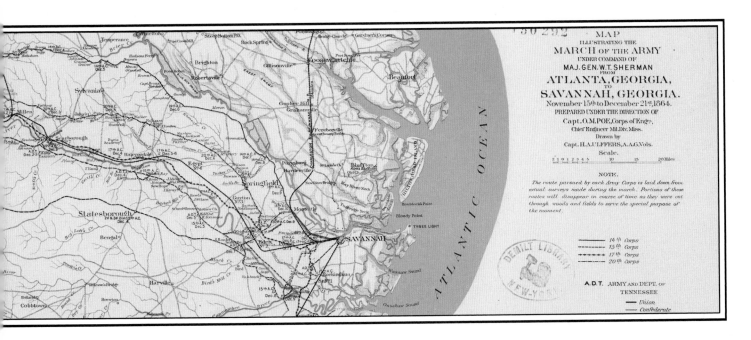

the Union force waited at Nashville, General John Schofield with thirty thousand men withdrew slowly as Hood advanced, and made a stand at Franklin, a town on the Harpeth River twenty miles south of Nashville. Angry at what he considered a lack of aggressive spirit in his army, the impetuous Hood decided against the advice of his subordinates to launch a frontal assault on the well-entrenched North. Without artillery preparation, Hood sent his men on the Indian summer afternoon of November 30 across a half mile of open ground with the rebel yell in their throats—for the last time. It was a slaughter. No fewer than twelve Confederate generals and fifty-four regimental commanders became casualties. Six generals were killed, including Patrick Cleburne.

Hood should have retreated while he still had an army. But he shared with Jefferson Davis the delusion that victory was still possible. He moved on toward Nashville, where on December 15 and 16 Thomas's full force attacked Hood's dispirited troops on the hills south of the city. The Army of Tennessee, the Confederacy's second army, melted away before this crushing onslaught. Hood resigned in January. Of the fifty thousand infantry he had inherited from Johnston in July, fewer than fifteen thousand men were left.

A new, more ominous style of warfare came in 1864. From Shiloh to Atlanta, General William Tecumseh Sherman, Uncle Billy as he was known to his troops, proved continually the need to go beyond the usual military bounds to end the war. After the fall of Atlanta, Sherman devised a campaign to break not only the army, but also the *spirit* of the South. On November 16, 1864, as fires raged through Atlanta, Sherman and his soldiers cut their ties to the North and headed eastward to the sea. The old ways were abandoned as total war erupted, forging a path sixty miles wide through Georgia. The march to the sea bled the already staggering Confederacy to death and proved, as Sherman was the first to say, that "war is hell."

The Battle of Franklin was the finale of John Bell Hood's vain hope to crush the Northern hold on Nashville. The results were disastrous: unsupported, uncoordinated attacks against a strongly entrenched Union line shattered the last Confederate hopes in Tennessee. Among the five generals to fall that day, Patrick Cleburne, the Irish immigrant lawyer from Arkansas who had risen to division command, was shot down as he led his men forward. His division, broken and battered, was now only a shadow of what it had once been—the finest in the Confederate army in the west. "If we are to die," Cleburne said that fateful day, "let us die like men." The following day, December 1, 1864, Cleburne's soldiers bore the body of their commander from the area on the Carter Plantation where he fell.

News of Hood's defeat produced "the darkest and most dismal day" of the Confederacy's short history, in the words of a Southern diarist. "The deep waters are closing over us," wrote another. But worse was yet to come. Lee's army drew its dwindling supplies from the Carolinas and through the port of Wilmington, North Carolina, the only port still accessible to blockade runners. That was because the mouth of the Cape Fear River below Wilmington was guarded by massive Fort Fisher, whose big guns kept blockade ships at bay and protected the runners. The Union navy had long wanted to attack Fort Fisher and shut this back door to Richmond. But diversions of army troops and naval ships to the long and futile campaign against Charleston had postponed the effort to capture Fort Fisher. In January 1865, however, the largest armada of the war, fifty-eight ships with six hundred and twenty-seven guns, blitzed the fort for two days, disabling most of its big guns. The fleet landed two thousand sailors and marines who attacked the fort's seaward face, while five thousand army troops circled around to the rear and swarmed over

Wilmington, North Carolina, defended by the extensive Fort Fisher, was the last open port on the Atlantic coast. Union naval and land forces finally stormed the fort in January 1865. At the height of the battle, Colonel Newton Curtis led his troops into Shepherd's Battery in the fort's northwest corner. As the last remaining gunner prepared to fire a loaded piece, it was the towering colonel himself who struck the man down. For his leadership and personal bravery, Curtis was promoted to the rank of brigadier general.

the parapets. The capture of the fort effectively ended blockade running.

And two weeks later Sherman's destroyers started north from Savannah, burning with a desire for revenge on South Carolina, which to their mind had started the war by seceding first and attacking Fort Sumter. The soldiers made even less distinction between civilian and military property than they had in Georgia. They "would sometimes stop to tell me that they were sorry for the women and children," wrote a woman whose house was plundered, "but South Carolina must be *destroyed*. South Carolina and her sins was the burden of their song." A pillaging private put it succinctly: "Here is where treason began, and, by God, here is where it shall end." Sherman's men left less of Columbia standing than they had left of Atlanta. This invincible army pushed into North Carolina and brushed aside the force Joseph Johnston, restored to command, had assembled to try to stop them. Behind them they left a longer trail of greater devastation than in Georgia. "All is gloom, despondency, and inactivity," wrote a South Carolina physician. "Our army is demoralized and the people panic-stricken. To fight longer seems to be madness."

But the war would not end until Confederate armies surrendered. Lincoln made this clear in his second inaugural address on March 4, 1865. The best-known words from this address urged a binding up of the nation's wounds "with malice toward none" and "charity for all." But of more significance in the midst of the still ongoing conflict were these words: "American slavery is one of those offences which, in the providence of God . . . He now wills to remove [through] this terrible war, as the woe due to those by whom the offence came. . . . Fondly do we hope—fervently do we pray—that this mighty scourge of war may speedily pass away. Yet if God wills that it continue, until all the wealth piled by the bondman's two hundred and fifty years of unrequited toil shall be sunk, and until every drop of blood drawn with the lash, shall be paid by another drawn with the sword, as was said three thousand years ago, so still it must be said, 'the judgments of the Lord are true and righteous altogether.' "

But Ulysses S. Grant did not intend the war to last that long. He knew that the Army of Northern Virginia—the only remaining entity that kept the Confederacy alive—was on the verge of disintegration. Scores of its soldiers were deserting every day. On April 1 Sheridan's cavalry (which had returned from the Valley) and the 5th Infantry Corps smashed the right flank of Lee's line at Five Forks and cut the last railroad into Petersburg from the South. The next day Grant attacked all along the line and forced Lee to abandon Petersburg. That night the army and government also evacuated Richmond after blowing up or setting afire all military stores. The fires spread and burned more of the Confederate capital than the Yankees had burned of Atlanta or Columbia.

Lee's starving men limped westward, hoping to turn south and join the remnants of Johnston's army in North Carolina. But Sheridan's cavalry raced ahead to cut them off while the Union infantry kept on Lee's flank and rear to hem them in. On April 6 at Sayler's Creek near Farmville, the Union sliced off one-quarter of the Army of Northern Virginia, pitched into them, and captured eight thousand Confederates including six generals. "My God!" exclaimed a stunned Robert E. Lee as he watched the climax of this action. "Has the army been dissolved?"

On the evening of March 4, 1865, at his second inaugural ball, according to newspaper accounts, President Lincoln, accompanied by his wife Mary, shook hands with more than six thousand people.

Not yet, but it soon would be. On April 8 Sheridan got in front of what was left of Lee's army at Appomattox Station, one hundred miles from Petersburg, and captured two trainloads of rations that had stood between the Army of Northern Virginia and starvation. When the weary Southerners tried a breakout attack next morning, their first probe revealed Union infantry in solid ranks behind the cavalry. It was the end. "There is nothing left for me to do," said Lee, "but to go and see General Grant, and I would rather die a thousand deaths."

Go he did, to the house of Wilmer McLean in the village of Appomattox Courthouse where Lee met Grant to surrender his troops. For the third time Grant had captured an entire enemy army. He gave generous terms, paroling officers and men alike to go home and take their horses with them "to put in a crop" and begin the recovery of the shattered South.

Lee was depressed as he rode away from McLean's house to inform his soldiers that their war was over. Curiously enough, Grant also felt "sad and depressed" as he watched Lee go, reflecting on "the downfall of a foe who had fought so long and valiantly, and had suffered so much for a cause, though that cause was, I believe, one of the worst for which a people ever fought."

As the Appomattox campaign ground through its fifth day, a third of Lee's battered army was cornered at Saylor's Creek, Virginia. Beyond the battlefield, an anxious Lee waited at Rice's Station with the remainder of his troops. As the refugees from the battle appeared, the usually composed Lee nearly broke down, exclaiming to himself, "My God! Has the army been dissolved?" Quickly recovering, the general picked up a battle flag and rode among the panicked men, rallying them with soothing words and his own composed presence. This was the last, dramatic rally of the Army of Northern Virginia.

General Lee rode slowly away from the tiny village of Appomattox Courthouse. He now had to face those who trusted him—the soldiers who followed him for four years. General A. L. Long, Lee's biographer and former aide wrote, "Hundreds of devoted veterans pressed around the noble chief, trying to take his hand, touch his person, or even lay a hand upon his horse, thus exhibiting for him their great affection." His cheeks damp with tears, Lee removed his hat and bade them farewell.

If Grant felt sad, he was almost the only Northerner who did. When news of Lee's surrender reached the North, coming hard upon the heels of Richmond's fall, unprecedented celebrations broke out. On Wall Street, of all places, "men embraced and hugged each other, *kissed* each other, retreated into doorways to dry their eyes and came out again to flourish their hats and hurrah," wrote a New York diarist. "They sang 'Old Hundred,' 'the Doxology,' 'John Brown,' and 'The Star-Spangled Banner' over and over, with a massive roar of the crowd and a unanimous wave of hats at the end of each repetition." The feeling was all the more intense because "founded on memories of years of failure, all but hopeless, and the consciousness that national victory was at last secured."

And victory *was* secured. Although Jefferson Davis was fleeing southward calling for renewed dedication to the cause of independence, Lee's surrender ensured the surrender of the other fragments of Confederate armies. And Jefferson Davis himself was captured by Union cavalry in Georgia on May 10.

Before that happened, however, Northern celebrations had turned overnight into mourning. On the evening of April 14, the careworn Abraham Lincoln relaxed by attending a comedy at Ford's Theater. In the middle of the play John Wilkes Booth broke into Lincoln's box and shot the president fatally in the head. An aspiring young actor overshadowed by the greater fame of his father and older brother Edwin, Booth was a native of Maryland, a Confederate supporter, and a frustrated, unstable egotist who hated Lincoln for what he had done to Booth's beloved South. As he jumped from Lincoln's box to the stage and escaped out a back door, Booth shouted Virginia's state motto to the startled audience: *"Sic semper tyrannis."*

Thus the tragedy of the American Civil War, begun by the shot of a Southern partisan, ended in the tragedy of an assassin's bullet fired by another Southern partisan.

Swords Into Plowshares

EPILOGUE

ON MAY 23 AND 24, 1865, THE TWO PRINCIPAL UNION ARMIES, one hundred thousand strong each, strode in triumph down Pennsylvania Avenue from the Capitol past the White House in a Grand Review to celebrate victory and the restoration of the *United* States. Afterwards the Union veterans scattered to their homes for demobilization, but not before their home towns gave the conquering heroes a festive welcome. "When Johnny Comes Marching Home," a Civil War song, rang out again and again in hundreds of Northern communities during the summer of 1865.

No such triumphal welcome greeted Confederate soldiers as they made their way home in small groups, ragged and almost starving, forced to beg, even to steal food along the way in order to survive. Many Southern veterans came home to burned-out farm buildings, fields growing up in weeds, railroads without tracks, bridges, or rolling stock, towns and cities marked by stark chimneys standing amidst charred ruins. Planters and their sons returned in poverty to plantations without slaves, without crops, without fences, with scarcely any food. Yeoman farmers returned to patches of land barely kept going by the hard work and sacrifices of wives and children during the past four years. The experiment of secession had cost the South one-quarter of its white men ages eighteen to thirty-five, two-fifths of its livestock, half of its farm machinery, and two-thirds of its total property, including slaves. The survivors went to work, cheerlessly but with determination, to salvage as much as possible from the wreckage and to build a better future.

Eight years after Appomattox, Mark Twain assessed the impact of the Civil War: It had "uprooted institutions that were centuries old, changed the politics of a people, transformed the social life of half the country, and wrought so profoundly upon the entire national character that the influence cannot be measured short of two or three generations." Before 1861 the words "United States" were a plural noun: "The United States *are* a large country." Since 1865 the United States *is* a singular noun. The North went to war to preserve the Union; it ended by creating a nation. This transformation can be traced in Lincoln's wartime addresses. His first inaugural address contained the word *Union* twenty times and the word *nation* not once. In Lincoln's first message to Congress, on July 4, 1861, he used *Union* thirty-two times and *nation* only three times. In his famous public letter to Horace Greeley of August 22, 1861, concerning slavery and the war, Lincoln spoke of the *Union* eight times and the *nation* not at all. But in the Gettysburg address fifteen months later, he did not refer to the *Union* at all but used the word *nation* five times. And in the second inaugural address, looking back over the trauma of the past four years, Lincoln spoke of one side seeking to dissolve the *Union* in 1861 and the other side accepting the challenge of war to preserve the *nation*.

The decentralized antebellum republic, in which the post office was the only agency of national government that touched the average citizen, was transformed by the crucible of war into a centralized polity that taxed people directly and created an internal revenue bureau to collect the taxes, expanded the jurisdiction of federal courts, created a national currency and a federally chartered banking system, drafted men into the army, and (in 1865) created a Freedmen's Bureau as the first national agency for social welfare. Eleven of the first twelve amendments to the Constitution had limited the powers of the national government; six of the next seven, starting with the Thirteenth Amendment in 1865, radically expanded those powers at the expense of the states. The first three of these postwar amendments transformed four million slaves into citizens and voters within five years, the most rapid and fundamental social transformation in American history—even if the nation did backslide on part of this commitment for three generations after 1877.

From 1789 to 1861, Southern slaveholders had been presidents of the United States two-thirds of the time; two-thirds of the speakers of the House and presidents pro tem of the Senate had also been Southerners. Twenty of the thirty-five Supreme Court justices during that period had been from the South, which always had a majority on the Court before 1861. After the Civil War, a century passed before another resident of a Southern state was elected president. For half a century after the war no Southerner served as speaker of the House or president pro tem of the Senate, and only five of the twenty-six Supreme Court justices appointed during that half-century were Southerners.

The institutions and ideology of a plantation society and a slave system that had dominated half of the country before 1861 and sought to dominate more went down with a great crash in 1865 and were replaced by the institutions and ideology of free-labor entrepreneurial capitalism. For better or for worse, the flames of civil war forged the framework of modern America.

THE IMAGES

The War Between the States (page 1)
1957
Opaque watercolor
17 × 14½ inches
Collection: Mr. George Tyler

Battle Above the Clouds (pages 2–3 and 126–127)
Lookout Mountain, Tennessee, November 24, 1863
1992
Oil on canvas
22 × 35 inches
Collection: Hammer Galleries, New York City

The Blue and the Gray (page 5)
1982
Opaque watercolor
12 × 18 inches
Collection: Mr. John P. Rafter

"The Bloody Angle" (pages 6–7)
Gettysburg, Pennsylvania, July 3, 1863
1988
Oil on canvas
18 × 24 inches
Collection: Mr. and Mrs. Michael L. Sharpe

Veterans of Gettysburg (pages 10–11)
1982
Oil on canvas
16 × 20 inches
Collection: Mr. Thomas Huff

Her Name Was Sojourner Truth (page 16)
1977
Oil on board
20¾ × 17½ inches
Collection: Mrs. Deborah Ann Künstler

The Lincoln-Douglas Debates (pages 20–21)
1987
Oil on canvas
30 × 30 inches
Collection: Mr. José Pires

Florida Secedes (pages 24–25)
January 10, 1861
1990
Oil on board
10 × 11¼ inches
Collection of the artist

The Flag and the Union Imperiled (pages 28–29)
Fort Sumter
1978
Oil on board
16⅛ × 18 inches
Collection: Mr. Homer Noble

First to the Guns (pages 36–37)
The Battle of Wilson's Creek, August 10, 1861
1992
Oil on canvas
18 × 30 inches
Collection: Hammer Galleries, New York City

"There Stands Jackson Like a Stone Wall" (pages 40–41)
General Thomas J. Jackson at First Manassas, July 21, 1861
1991
Oil on canvas
24 × 36 inches
Collection: Hammer Galleries, New York City

The Waiting War (pages 44–45)
1982
Opaque watercolor
15½ × 19 inches
Collection: Mr. John Edwards

The Monitor and the Merrimack (pages 46–47)
Hampton Roads, Virginia, March 9, 1862
1985
Oil on board
12 × 14 inches
Collection: American Print Gallery, Gettysburg, Pennsylvania

The Ghost Column (pages 52–53)
Colonel Nathan Bedford Forrest leaves Fort Donelson,
Tennessee, February 16, 1862
1991
Oil on canvas
22 × 30 inches
Collection: Hammer Galleries, New York City

The Fight at Fallen Timbers (pages 56–57)
Forrest and Morgan at Shiloh, April 8, 1862
1991
Oil on canvas
22 × 36 inches
Collection: Hammer Galleries, New York City

"Until We Meet Again" (pages 62–63)
Jackson's headquarters, Winchester, Virginia, Winter 1862
1990
Oil on canvas
30 × 46 inches
Collection: Farmers and Merchants National Bank, Winchester, Virginia

Confederate Winter (pages 64–65)
General Taylor at Swift Run Gap, Virginia, March 1862
1989
Oil on canvas
28 × 42 inches
Collection: Mr. Stacy B. Lloyd III

General "Stonewall" Jackson Enters Winchester, Virginia (pages 68–69)
May 25, 1862
1988
Oil on canvas
30 × 48 inches
Collection: Farmers and Merchants National Bank, Winchester, Virginia

Morgan's Raiders (pages 74–75)
Alexandria, Tennessee, December 21, 1862
1982
Oil on canvas
25 × 40 inches
Collection: Mr. Milton Turner

Jackson at Antietam (Sharpsburg) (pages 80–81)
General "Stonewall" Jackson, September 17, 1862, Dunker Church
1989
Oil on canvas
32 × 50 inches
Collection: U.S. Army War College, Carlisle, Pennsylvania

"Raise the Colors and Follow Me" (pages 82–83)
The Irish Brigade at Antietam, September 17, 1862
1991
Oil on canvas
30 × 44 inches
Collection: U.S. Army War College, Carlisle, Pennsylvania

Lee at Fredericksburg (pages 86–87)
Princess Anne Street, 9:40 A.M., November 20, 1862
1990
Oil on canvas
34 × 56 inches
Collection: Mr. and Mrs. Michael L. Sharpe

Emancipation Proclamation (page 88)
1987
Oil on canvas
30 × 30 inches
Collection: Mr. and Mrs. Michael L. Sharpe

Grierson's Butternut Guerrillas (pages 94–95)
Newton Station, Mississippi, April 24, 1863
1991
Oil on canvas
28 × 38 inches
Collection: Hammer Galleries, New York City

The Glorious Fourth (pages 98–99)
General Ulysses S. Grant at Vicksburg, July 4, 1863
1989
Oil on canvas
34 × 56 inches
Collection: Mr. and Mrs. Michael L. Sharpe

The Last Council (pages 100–101)
Jackson, Lee, and Stuart at Chancellorsville, May 1, 1863
1990
Oil on canvas
28 × 36 inches
Collection: Hammer Galleries, New York City

The Grand Review (pages 104–105)
Brandy Station, Virginia, June 5, 1863
1989
Oil on canvas
38 × 44 inches
Collection: Hammer Galleries, New York City

"Oh, I Wish He Was Ours" (pages 106–107)
Hagerstown, Maryland, June 26, 1863
1991
Oil on canvas
24 × 32 inches
Collection: Hammer Galleries, New York City

"There's the Devil to Pay" (pages 108–109)
General John Buford at Gettysburg, July 1, 1863
1990
Oil on canvas
30 × 54 inches
Collection: U.S. Army War College, Carlisle, Pennsylvania

Dilger at Gettysburg (pages 110–111)
July 1, 1863
1989
Oil on canvas
28 × 42 inches
Collection: Mr. Pat Kilbane

The Grandest Charge Ever Seen (pages 114–115)
Barksdale's Mississippians at Gettysburg, July 2, 1863
1990
Oil on canvas
26 × 48 inches
Collection: Hammer Galleries, New York City

The High Water Mark (pages 116–117)
Gettysburg, July 3, 1863
1988
Oil on canvas
34 × 56 inches
Collection: Mr. and Mrs. Harold Bernstein

"It's All My Fault" (pages 118–119)
General Robert E. Lee at Gettysburg, July 3, 1863
1989
Oil on canvas
26 × 48 inches
Collection: Mr. Thorne Donnelly, Jr.

Eye of the Storm (pages 122–123)
Patrick Cleburne at Chickamauga, September 20, 1863
1991
Oil on canvas
26 × 35 inches
Collection: Hammer Galleries, New York City

Colonel Robert Shaw and the 54th Massachusetts (pages 128–129)
Boston, Massachusetts, May 28, 1863
1991
Oil on canvas
16 × 20 inches
Collection: Hammer Galleries, New York City

The Gettysburg Address (pages 130–131)
1987
Oil on canvas
30 × 30 inches
Collection: Mr. and Mrs. Harold Bernstein

The Thirteenth Amendment is Passed (page 133)
1982
Oil on canvas
10 × 11½ inches
Collection: American Print Gallery, Gettysburg, Pennsylvania

Last Leave (pages 136–137)
1982
Oil on canvas
16 × 20 inches
Collection: Ms. Julianne J. Attebury

"On to Richmond" (pages 140–141)
Grant in the Wilderness, May 7, 1864
1991
Oil on canvas
30 × 42 inches
Collection: U.S. Army War College, Carlisle, Pennsylvania

The Bloody Angle (pages 144–145)
Spotsylvania, Virginia, May 12, 1864
1991
Oil on canvas
24 × 36 inches
Collection: Hammer Galleries, New York City

Sheridan's Men (pages 146–147)
1982
Oil on board
22¾ × 30 inches
Collection: Mr. and Mrs. Ray Wayman

Battle for the Shenandoah (pages 152–153)
1982
Oil on canvas
28¼ × 40 inches
Collection: Jerrine Lovitt

"War is Hell" (pages 156–157)
General William Tecumseh Sherman, Atlanta, November 15, 1864
1991
Oil on canvas
30 × 38 inches
Collection: Hammer Galleries, New York City

Bringing Cleburne In (pages 158–159)
Franklin, Tennessee, December 1, 1864
1991
Oil on canvas
24 × 36 inches
Collection: Hammer Galleries, New York City

The Gunner and the Colonel (pages 160–161)
The Battle of Fort Fisher, January 15, 1865
1992
Oil on canvas
24 × 42 inches
Collection: Hammer Galleries, New York City

Lincoln's Inaugural Ball (page 163)
1987
Oil on canvas
30 × 30 inches
Collection: Mr. José Pires
Collection: Hammer Galleries, New York City

The Last Rally (pages 164–165)
Sayler's Creek, Virginia, April 6, 1865
1991
Oil on canvas
22 × 34 inches
Collection: Hammer Galleries, New York City

"We Still Love You Just As Much as Ever, General Lee" (pages 166–167)
Appomattox, Virginia, April 9, 1865
1989
Oil on canvas
26 × 42 inches
Collection: Robert E. Mullane

"...Swords into Plowshares" (pages 170–171)
1991
Oil on canvas
20 × 26 inches
Collection: Hammer Galleries, New York City

Still Flying (page 173)
1982
Opaque watercolor
17 × 14½ inches
Collection: Mrs. William Ford

Private Harrison Hunt, 119 Regiment, N.Y.S.V. (page 8)
1982
Oil on canvas
14 × 12 inches
Collection: Mr. Robert E. Mullane

Jefferson Davis (page 12)
President of the Confederacy
1990
Oil on board
10 × 11½ inches
Collection of the artist

General William Barksdale (page 23)
1990
Oil on board
10 × 11½ inches
Collection of the artist

General Pierre Beauregard (page 27)
1991
Oil on board
10 × 11⅜ inches
Collection of the artist

General Robert E. Lee (pages 30–31)
1991
Oil on board
10 × 11½ inches
Collection of the artist

Colonel Zebulon B. Vance (page 33)
1991
Oil on board
10 × 11½ inches
Collection of the artist

General John Sappington Marmaduke (page 35)
1990
Oil on board
10 × 11½ inches
Collection of the artist

General George McClellan (page 43)
1990
Oil on board
10 × 11½ inches
Collection of the artist

Admiral David Glasgow Farragut (page 58)
1990
Oil on board
10 × 11½ inches
Collection of the artist

General Thomas "Stonewall" Jackson (pages 60–61)
1991
Oil on board
10 × 11½ inches
Collection of the artist

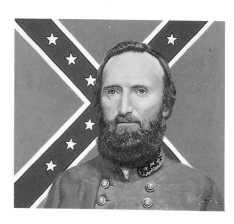

Thaddeus Lowe and His Balloon (page 67)
1991
Oil on board
10 × 11½ inches
Collection of the artist

General J. E. B. Stuart (page 70)
1991
Oil on board
10 × 11½ inches
Collection of the artist

General John Hunt Morgan (page 72)
1990
Oil on board
10 × 11½ inches
Collection of the artist

General Ulysses S. Grant (pages 90–91)
1990
Oil on board
10 × 11½ inches
Collection of the artist

Admiral David Porter (page 93)
1990
Oil on board
10 × 11¼ inches
Collection of the artist

General James Longstreet (page 112)
1990
Oil on board
10 × 11¼ inches
Collection of the artist

General John Bell Hood (page 120)
1991
Oil on board
10 × 11⅜ inches
Collection of the artist

President Abraham Lincoln (pages 134–135)
1991
Oil on board
10 × 11⅜ inches
Collection of the artist

General William Tecumseh Sherman (page 138)
1991
Oil on board
10 × 11½ inches
Collection of the artist

General John Brown Gordon (page 142)
1990
Oil on board
10 × 11½ inches
Collection of the artist

General Nathan Bedford Forrest (page 150)
1991
Oil on board
10 × 11½ inches
Collection of the artist

President Abraham Lincoln (page 169)
1991
Opaque watercolor
4½ × 4½ inches
Collection: American Print Gallery, Gettysburg, Pennsylvania

INDEX

Boldface references denote illustrations.

Abolitionism, 17-18
Alabama, 46
"Anaconda Plan, The," 38
Anderson, "Bloody Bill," 33
Anderson, Robert, 26, 29
Andrew, John, 129
Antietam, battle of, 79, **80-81**, 82, **82-83**, **84**, 85
Appomattox, surrender at, 164, **166-167**, 168
Arkansas, 32, 34, 54
Army of Northern Virginia, 71, 85, 162, **164-165**
Army of Tennessee, 89, 121, 157
Army of the Cumberland, 89, 121, 124
Army of the Potomac, 38, 59, 66-67, 73, 76, 82, 139
Army of the Shenandoah, **146-147**, 151, **152-153**
Army of Virginia, 73
Atlanta
   battle of, 148
   burning of, **156-157**
   capture of, 149, 151
Atlantic Monthly, 131

Balloon corps, 67, 71
Banks, Nathaniel, 68
Barksdale, William, 20, **23**, 112, **114-115**
Battle above the Clouds, 124, **126-127**
Beauregard, Pierre G. T., 26, **27**, 38, 51
Benton, **98-99**
Black regiment (54th Massachusetts Infantry), **128-129**, 129, 131
Blockades, 42
Bloody Angle of Spotsylvania, 143, 144
Bloody Lane, 82
Booth, John Wilkes, 168
Bragg, Braxton, 73, 74, 76, 79, 89, 121, 127
Brandy Station, battle of, 103
Buell, Don Carlos, 51, 54, 89
Buford, John, 106, 108, **108-109**
Bull Run, battle of, 38, 79

Burnside, Ambrose, 46, 79, 82, 85, 92
"Bushwackers," 33
Butler, Benjamin, 76, 78

Calhoun, John C., 18
Camp life, **44-45**
Carmody, John, **28-29**
Casualties, 9, 32-34, 51, 54, 71, 82, 85, 103, 116, 124, 139, 146, 148
Cedar Creek, battle of, 151, 153
Cedar Mountain, battle of, 73, 78-79
Cemetary Ridge, battle of, 116
Chancellorsville, battle of, 96, **100-101**, 101, **102**, 103
Charleston Mercury, 18, 149
Chattanooga, capture of, 124, **126-127**, 127
Chestnut, Mary Boykin, 127
Chickamauga, battle of, **122-123**, 123-124, **125**
Civil War Round Tables, 9
Cleburne, Patrick, **122-123**, 124, 157, 158, **158-159**
Compromise of 1850, 19
Confederate Congress, 32
Confederate Constitution, 22
Confiscation acts, 78
Constitutional View of the War between the States, A (Stephens), 15
"Contrabands," 78
Corinth, Mississippi, 51, 54, 73
Cotton gin, 15, 17
Cumberland River, **49**, 50, 51
Curtis, Newton, **160-161**
Custer, George Armstrong, 153

Davis, Jefferson, **12**, 17, 20, 62
   captured by Union cavalry, 168
   decides to start war, 26
   elected president of Confederacy, 22
   inaugural address, 22
   replaces Bragg, 127
   replaces Johnston, 148
   on secession, 14-15

Delaware, 33
Democratic party, 20, 22, 78, 85, 92, 127, 132, 148, 149
Dilger, Hubert, 108, **110-111**
"Dixie," 22
Douglas, Stephen A., 19-20, **20-21**
Douglass, Frederick, 17, 129
Dred Scott decision (1857), 19-20

Early, Jubal, 149, 151, 153, 154
Emancipation Proclamation, 76, 78, 85, **88**, 89, 127, 131, 132
Ewell, Richard, 64, 108

Farragut, David Glasgow, 54, **58**, 59
Fisher's Hill, battle of, 151, 153
Florida, 46
Forrest, Nathan Bedford, 50-51, **52-53**, 54, **56-57**, 73, 149, **150**
Fort Donelson, capture of, 50, 51
Fort Fisher, capture of, 160, **160-161**, 162
Fort Henry, capture of, 50
Fort Sumter, capture of, 26, **28-29**, 32
Fort Wagner, battle of, 129, 131
France, 76, 85
Franklin, battle of, 157, **158-159**
Frederick, Maryland, 79
Fredericksburg, Virginia, **86-87**
Freedman's Bureau, 172
Fugitive Slave Law of 1850, 15
Furloughs, **136-137**

Gaines' Mill, battle of, 71
Garrison, William Lloyd, 17, 18
Georgia, 139, 148, 149, 151, 154-155, **154-155**
Gettysburg, battle of, **10-11**, 106, 108, **108-109**, **110-111**, 112, **113**, **114-115**, 116, **116-117**, **118-119**
Gettysburg address, 10, **130-131**, 131-132, 172

Gordon, John Brown, **142**, 143
Gorgas, Josiah, 42, 121
Grant, Ulysses S., **90**
  accepts surrender by Lee, 164
  appointed general in chief, 127
  attacks Forts Henry and
    Donelson, 50-51
  on Lee, 164
  at Petersburg, 146
  at Shiloh, 51, 54
  at Spotsylvania, 139, 143, 144
  strategy for 1864, 136, 139
  in Vicksburg campaign, 85,
    92-94, 96, **98-99**
  at The Wilderness, 139,
    140-141
Great Britain, 76, 85
Greeley, Horace, 149
Grierson, Benjamin, 93-94
Gunboats, 45, **46-47**, 48, 50, 51,
  54, 59, 92-93

Halleck, Henry W., 54
Hampton, Wade, 146
Harper's Ferry, battle of, 79, **84**
Hill, A. P., 82
H. L. Hunley, **48**
Hood, John Bell, **120**, 121, 123,
  124, 148, 149, 155, 157, 158
Hooker, Joseph "Fighting Joe," 79,
  92, 96, 101, 103, 124
Hunt, Harrison, 98

Irish Brigade, Army of the
  Potomac, 82, **82-83**
Ironclad warships, **46-47**, 48

Jackson, Mary Ann, **62-63**
Jackson, Thomas J. "Stonewall,"
  59, **61**, 62-63
  at Antietam, 79, **80-81**
  at Bull Run, 38
  at Cedar Mountain, 73
  at Chancellorsville, **100-101**, 101,
    103
  character of, 62, 64
  at Kernstown, 64
  at second battle of Manassas, 73,
    76
  at Seven Days battles, 71
  in Shenandoah Valley campaign,
    62-63, 64, 66, 67, **68-69**
James, Frank, 33
James, Jesse, 33
"Jayhawkers," 33
Jefferson, Thomas, 18

Johnston, Albert Sidney, 51, 162
Johnston, Joseph E., 38, 62, 71,
  94, 96, 127, 146, 148,
Jonesboro, battle of, 149

Kearsarge, 46
Kentucky, 33, **49**, 50, 51, 73, 74,
  76, 78, 79
Kernstown, battle of, 64

Lee, Robert E., **31**, 59, **106-107**
  at Chancellorsville, 96, **100-101**,
    101, 103
  on decision to join Confederate
    Army, 32
  first field command, 62
  in Fredericksburg, **86-87**
  at Gettysburg, 106, 108, 112, 116,
    118-119
  invasion of Maryland and, 76
  at Petersburg, 146
  at Saylor's Creek, 162, **164-165**
  at Seven Days battles, 71
  in Shenandoah Valley campaign,
    64
  at Spotsylvania, 139, 143
  strategy for 1864, 136
  surrenders, 164, 168
  with troops after surrender,
    166-167
  at The Wilderness, 139
Liberator, The, 17
Lincoln, Abraham, **135**, 169
  anti-slavery policy, 15, 19-20
  appeals to nationalism of
    Southerners, 25
  appoints Grant general in chief,
    127
  assassination of, 168
  balloon corps and, 67
  on battle of Chancellorsville, 103
  on black soldiers, 131
  blockade policy, 42
  calls for volunteer militia, 32
  debates with Douglas, 19-20,
    20-21
  decision for war or peace and, 26
  on 1864 election, 149
  Emancipation Proclamation, 76,
    78, 85, **88**, 89
  Gettysburg address, 10, **130-131**,
    131-132, 172
  on Grant, 92, 96
  "House Divided" speech, 19
  inaugural addresses, 26, 162, 172
  insists on maintaining Union, 25
  on Lee's escape from
    Gettysburg, 116
  reelected President, 154

replaces Buell, 89
  replaces Burnside, 92
  replaces McClellan, 76
  Rosencrans and, 89
  at second inaugural ball, **163**
  on slavery, 10, 20
Lincoln, Mary Todd, **163**
London Times, 32
Long, A. L., 167
Longstreet, James, 76, **86-87**, 96,
  103, **112**, 121, 124, 136
Lookout Mountain, battle of, 124,
  126-127
Lowe, Thaddeus, 67, **67**
Lyon, Nathaniel, 34

Malvern Hill, battle of, 71
Manassas, battles of, 38, 73, 76
Maps, **39**, **49**, **55**, **77**, **84**, **97**, **102**,
  113, **125**, **154-155**
Marmaduke, John Sappington,
  34, **35**
Marshall, Charles, **118-119**
Maryland, 33, 34, 76, 78
McClellan, George B., 35, 73, 154
  at Antietam, 79, 82, 85
  nominated for president, 149
  replaced by Burnside as
    commander, 85
  in Richmond campaign, 59, 64,
    66-67, 71
McColloh, Ben, 36
McDowell, Irvin, 38
McIntosh, James, **36-37**
McLean, Wilbur, 164
Meade, George Gordon, 108, 112,
  116, 139, 144
Meagher, Thomas Francis, **82-83**
Memphis, Tennessee, 54
Merrimack, 45, 46, 48
Merritt, Wesley, 153
Missouri, 33-34, 78
Missouri Compromise 1820, 19
Monitor, **46-47**, 48
Morgan, John Hunt, 57, **72**, 73,
  74-75
"Mud March," 92
Murfreesboro, battle of, 89

Nashville, Tennessee, 51
Naval warfare, 42-46, **46-47**, 48,
  49, 50-51, 54, 59, 92-93, 160,
  162
New Orleans, Louisiana, 54, 59
Newton Station, Mississippi, 94,
  94-95
New York Tribune, The, 59, 131
New York World, 148
North Carolina, 32

Ohio River, 49, 50

Pea Ridge, battle of, 54
Pemberton, John C., 94, 96
Perryville, battle of, 73, 89
Petersburg, battle of, 146
Pickett, George, 112
Pickett's charge, 112, **116-117**
Pittsburg Landing, battle of, *see*
　Shiloh, battle of
Pope, John, 54, 73
Porter, David D., 54, 92-93, **93**, 99
Porter, Horace, 141
Port Hudson, surrender of, 96, 121
Port Royal Sound, 45, 62

Quantrill, William, 33

Republican party, 19, 22, 78, 131,
　132
Reynolds, John, 108, **108-109**
Rhodes, James Ford, 14
Richmond, Virginia, 32, 38, 59, 64,
　66-67, 71
Richmond Examiner, 151
Rosencrans, William S., 74, 89,
　121, 124

Savannah, capture of, 155
Saylor's Creek, battle of, 162
Schofield, John, 157
Scott, Winfield, 35, 38
Secession, 14-15, 22
Semmes, Raphael, 46
Seven Days battles, 71
Seven Pines, battle of, 71
Seward, William H., 19, 78

Sharpsburg, battle of, 79, **80-81**,
　82, **82-83**, 84
Shaw, Robert Gould, **128-129**, 129,
　131
Shenandoah Valley campaigns, 62,
　64, **64-65**, 66, 67, **68-69**, 151,
　152-153
Sheridan, Philip, 143, **146-147**, 151,
　153, 162, 164
Sherman, William Tecumseh, 124,
　136, **138**
　captures Atlanta, 149, 151
　Confederate retreat after battle
　　of Shiloh and, 54, 57
　in Georgia campaigns, 139, 146,
　　148, 154-155, **156-157**
　on nature of war, 154
　in South Carolina campaign, 162
　in Vicksburg campaign, 89, 93
Shiloh, battle of, 51, 54, 55
Ship Island, 45
Sickles, Daniel, 115
Slavery
　abolitionism and, 17-18
　as cause of secession, 14-15, 17
　conflict over, 17-19
　Dred Scott decision and, 19-20
　Emancipation Proclamation and,
　　76, 78, 85, **88**, 89, 127, 131,
　　132
　Lincoln-Douglas debates and,
　　19-20
　Lincoln on, 10, 20
　Thirteenth Amendment and,
　　132, 172
South Carolina, 162
"Southern Rights" Democratic
　party, 20
Spotsylvania, battle of, 139, 143,
　144-145
Stanton, Edwin M., 67
States' rights argument for
　secession, 14-15
Stephens, Alexander H., 14, 15, *22*
Stones River, battle of, 89
Stuart, J. E. B., **70**, 71, **100-101**,
　103, **104-105**, 106, 143
Supreme Court, 15, 19, 172

Taylor, Richard, 64, **64-65**
Tennessee, 32, **49**, 50, 51, 54, 73,
　89, 154, 155
Tennessee River, **49**, 50, 51
Texas, annexation of, 19
Thirteenth Amendment, 132, 172
Thomas, George, 123, 124, 155
"Tinclad" gunboats, 50, 51
Truth, Sojourner, **16**, 17-18
Twain, Mark, 172

Vance, Zebulon B., **33**
Van Dorn, Earl, 73
Vicksburg, campaigns against, 59,
　85, 92-94, 96, **97**, **98-99**, 112
Virginia, 32, 38, 62, 64, 66, 67, 71,
　73, 92, 139
Virginia, **46-47**, 48

Warships, **46-47**, 48
Weed, Thurlow, 149
West Virginia, 34-35
Wheeler, "Fightin' Joe," 149
"When Johnny Comes Marching
　Home," 171
Wilderness, The, battle of, 139,
　140-141
Williamsburg, battle of, 66-67
Wilson's Creek, battle of, 34, **36-37**
Winchester, battle of, 66, **68-69**,
　151, 153
Winslow, John A., 46
Women's rights movement, 17

Yancey, William L., 22
Younger, Cole, 33
Younger, Jim, 33